ADVENTURES IN LARRYLAND!

LARRY ZBYSZKO

ECW Press

Copyright © Larry Zbyszko, 2008

Published by ECW Press
2120 Queen Street East, Suite 200,
Toronto, Ontario, Canada M4E 1E2
416.694.3348 / info@ecwpress.com

All rights reserved. No part of this publication may be reproduced, stored in a retrieval system, or transmitted in any form by any process — electronic, mechanical, photocopying, recording, or otherwise — without the prior written permission of the copyright owners and ECW Press.

LIBRARY AND ARCHIVES CANADA CATALOGUING IN PUBLICATION

Zbyszko, Larry
Adventures in Larryland! / Larry Zbyszko.

ISBN 978-1-55022-826-7

1. Zbyszko, Larry. 2. Wrestling. 3. Wrestlers — United — States Biography.
I. Title.

GV1196.Z39A3 2008 796.812092 C2007-907103-1

Editor: Michael Holmes
Cover Design: Dave Gee
Typesetting: Mary Bowness
Photo Insert and Production: Rachel Brooks
Cover Images: George Napolitano
Printing: Transcontinental

This book is set in Adobe Garamond and Trajan

PRINTED AND BOUND IN CANADA

ADVENTURES IN LARRYLAND!

TABLE OF CONTENTS

Acknowledgements

Where does one start when it took three decades and millions of people to make a dream come true? From loving parents, who tried their best to keep me from becoming a wrestler, to my best friend and wife, Kathleen, who, being the daughter of a famous wrestling promoter, knew better than to marry a wrestler but did so anyway.

Special thanks to a good friend and great guy, Scott Hudson, and his family, for letting me enjoy the seclusion of their mountain cabin where I disappeared for a month to write the first half of my book and for typing my manuscript which saved me about two years of suffering with my one-finger typing technique.

To young wrestlers like Chasyn Rance and Mister Saint Laurent of Team Vision who kept my enthusiasm high while finishing this book with a love and dedication to the wrestling business they will keep it alive for the next generation of fans.

I wonder sometimes what human beings would do if we didn't have heroes — someone to set forth a challenge and give us a purpose to achieve something greater. It seems inadequate to simply say thanks to someone you can't thank enough. To Bruno Sammartino who took me under his wing when it wasn't popular to do so: thanks, you'll always be my hero.

And to the millions of the wildest, craziest, and most dedicated fans on the planet without whom no wrestler's dreams would come true. I love you all.

Foreword

by Mike Tenay

I presume the age-old cliché "Work Smarter, Not Harder" has already been taken as a book title, but if not, it sure would apply to the wrestling life of Larry Zbyszko.

As an outsider, in the years before I was employed in the wrestling business, I had my opinion of Larry, the wrestler. Every time that I watched him compete in the squared circle I'd think about that cliché and marvel at his ability to get heat, to get a crowd reaction, by manipulating the fans. But what impressed me most was his method of getting that response. As I studied his MO, it became obvious that he would rather use his brains than his brawn. He would just as soon entertain by putting together a stinging monologue directed at ringsiders, whom he dubbed "the spudheads," than putting together a series of physical high spots that he would regret in his retirement years. Yes, Larry, the accomplished amateur wrestler who earned awards as a professional from the toughest critics, had outsmarted us all.

In addition to his in-ring ability, Zbyszko had earned a reputation as one of the best talkers in wrestling. His condescending interviews grew out of his most famous wrestling moment, his attack on his mentor, Bruno Sammartino, and he polished that abrasive style to perfection. So it was no surprise that Larry's wrestling career would have a second life analyzing the action as a color commentator on TV.

When I joined the WCW announcing team, I wasn't sure how I'd be greeted or treated. Would I be accepted into the fraternity or would I be frozen out? Would my background as a fan, writer and radio show host be looked at negatively because I wasn't a former wrestler? From the moment I began working with Larry Zbyszko and Bobby Heenan, I realized my concerns were unfounded. I was not only treated as an equal, I was invited into their social circle. With the hectic, year-round schedule of live TV events that were broadcast from all over the world, we would often joke that we spent more time together than we did with our families and that was when I formed my opinion of Larry, the person.

I can tell you that after years of dealing with almost every big-name wrestler in the profession, their real-life personalities are as varied as their onscreen characters. You never really know what you are going to get. But in a business of roller-coaster temperaments, Larry Zbyszko is as even-keeled as it gets. And in the high-pressure environment of producing a live television show, that balance is necessary. Away from the arena, Larry is one of those individuals who attracts the attention of everyone whose path he crosses. And in the past decade-plus that I've spent with him, we've had many great experiences. You've seen the countless hours of televised memorable moments, but off-air is when life with Larry is really entertaining.

In addition to live televised events, we would spend

hours in the studio doing voice-over work where we would announce previously taped matches. Larry would always enter the studio with a stack of lottery tickets and scratch-offs and I can recall him being so interested in hitting a payoff that we would be forced to bust the session because of his good fortune. In fact, Larry would combine gambling and wrestling by organizing a pool on the number of clotheslines that were used in each match. After deferring to my background in the Las Vegas gaming industry to come up with a "total" for each match, bets were placed by announcers, cameramen and audio engineers. Larry always insisted, "If Public Enemy is wrestling, bet the over!" During the commentary, Larry would openly refer to the number of clotheslines and often exclaim, "That's it . . . eleven puts it over the total," a comment that no one watching at home had a clue about.

I can recall an Atlanta–Las Vegas flight where I was recruited by WCW producer Keith Mitchell and Dusty Rhodes to educate Larry on the casino dice game of craps. Larry was looking to expand his gambling resumé outside of blackjack and poker and he, Keith and Dusty were going to try their luck at Binion's, one of the old school downtown casinos. Keith and Dusty clued me in that they had told Larry of the "can't miss" bet that only the locals know about . . . The $5 whoopee. Yes, as a former Nevada resident I spent the flight instructing Larry on a special wager where you holler "whoopee" at the top of your lungs when tossing the dice. Can you imagine the reaction from the grizzled cigar smokers hunched around the dice table when Larry let loose with a yell?

Larry would go out of his way to tell me his secrets to surviving "twenty-plus glorious years" in wrestling. One time I can remember him standing nearby when the WCW boss, Eric Bischoff, asked me to grade the previous night's pay-per-view event. As I explained my grade of a 6+ on a scale of 1–10 to Bischoff, I could see the look of exasperation on the face of Zbyszko. The second that Eric walked away, Larry exclaimed, "What are you doing? A six? Remember, when the boss asks . . . It's hot . . . It's great . . . It's a ten!"

Getting to know Larry Zbyszko as a wrestler and an announcer and, even more importantly, as a person puts him on the list of the most unforgettable characters I've ever met. And as you can imagine, that covers some ground. Enjoy this book that documents his life and, you know, after reading it myself I have to admit, "It's hot . . . It's great . . . It's a ten!"

CHAPTER ONE

HUMBLE BEGINNINGS

Welcome to Larryland, the mythical residence of my alter ego, the Living Legend.

It all started more than thirty glorious years ago. I was raised as a child of the '50s, a time when cities became suburbs and black and white television sets became standard equipment in every living room across America.

I was totally brainwashed by my childhood idols: comic book heroes like Superman, the Lone Ranger, and one of my all-time favorites, Zorro. There was no doubt in my mind that saving the helpless from injustice, thwarting evil and winding up with the beautiful damsel in distress was what life was all about. In fact, the first thing I did to my first house was put in a secret door so I could be just like Don Diego. Man, was I screwed up. Nevertheless, by the time I was twelve I knew what I was destined to become. I was going to be a hero.

When my family moved to Pittsburgh from Chicago in 1964, the future I envisioned came into perfect focus. There he was, the embodiment of everything I wanted to be: a 5′11″ 270-pound gorilla named Bruno Sammartino, who tossed bad guys into the air and crushed the life out of evil with his deadly bear hug. There was no doubt in my mind that I could achieve my childhood dream if I emulated this guy. I'd protect the weak, stop evil in its tracks and fly above the real world just like Clark Kent. That's right, I was going to become a professional wrestler.

But being Polish, it just wasn't going to be easy.

So, when I turned sixteen, I became a stalker. I couldn't help it — when I found out my larger-than-life, living and breathing hero lived only two miles away, I had to drive past his house every chance I got. One day, I damn near wrecked my car. There he was in his backyard — I could see him through the hedges. I'm sure it made his day, some sixteen-year-old, pimply faced kid stumbling through his shrubbery. But that's how it started — I trespassed into his privacy. I introduced myself, very respectfully, and for some reason he bought my dream. It really was as simple as that — Bruno's protegé, Larry Zbyzsko, was born.

We started working out in Bruno's basement. In between the armbars, wristlocks and lessons in psychology, we lifted weights. *For three hours.* We spent an hour and a half just working on the chest. Man, was Bruno strong. He once held some record for bench pressing 565½ pounds with a body weight of 265. When I started working with him he was in his early forties and had suffered numerous injuries but he was still doing 505 pounds when I hit my best bench press at 435½ pounds (while weighing 240). During one workout, after reaching our maximum weights, we put 350 pounds on the bench just to see how many reps we could do.

I did nineteen.

Bruno did twenty-four — and he was two decades older than me.

They say you never forget your first match, and they're right.

Barely twenty-one, I was ready to go. All pumped up (without steroids), after years of amateur wrestling and martial arts, and now armed with the old school submission holds, I entered the Civic Arena in Pittsburgh and made my way to the ring like I was Bruno Sammartino himself. There I was, at the bottom of those three little steps, my stairway to heaven in the squared circle. I was a massive hunk of muscle, glowing under the lights — a killing machine. But I could hardly pick up a leg I was so nervous. I couldn't breathe, my mouth was dry, my heart was pounding and my muscles were absolute rubber. I looked around the arena. Standing there dumbstruck in front of thousands of strangers, I realized they were all dressed while I was wearing nothing but these stupid little trunks. It felt like I was in some kind of naked-in-front-of-the-whole-world nightmare. That first trip to the ring was absolutely horrifying. But then suddenly, my opponent, "Slip Mahoney" Dorso, attacked. Because of my great mentor, I subdued the wicked Dorso with two arm drags. Then I hoisted him up in the backbreaker, Bruno's finishing hold. Dorso submitted. The fans went berserk, blowing the roof off the arena. I was victorious — in just seventeen seconds. It couldn't have happened any other way: Bruno's protegé had just exploded onto the scene.

Feeling the energy, the emotional outburst of thousands of people in unison, I was hooked. I began to live to pop crowds. And I was never nervous again.

CHAPTER TWO

THE PROTEGÉ GIMMICK

Being a new, young talent that Bruno Sammartino himself brought into the business opened doors for me — doors that would have remained sealed to just about any other newcomer. Back then, professional wrestling's secret society did not want you anywhere near the business. Today, there are countless wrestling "schools" that will gladly take your money and invite you in. In the good old days of the territories — before Vince McMahon's WWF changed the landscape — wrestling had "policemen," guys who were there to keep you out.

When some wannabe showed up at an arena to pester somebody for a chance, they'd wind up in the ring that very afternoon with someone like Karl Gotch, Billy Robinson or some other heartless submission master. You know, just to see if they "had what it takes." Well, they never "had" anything, not even a chance. They would limp home, nursing their broken wrist or dislocated shoulder — proud as can be about being brutalized by their television hero, but never to be seen in the ring again.

Thanks to Bruno, I had a storybook entrance into this "closed shop." Almost from the beginning, the big stars of the time, from Chief Jay Strongbow to Killer Kowalski, as well as the most important agents, men like Arnold Skaaland, Gorilla Monsoon and Angelo Savoldi, treated me like I was family. They actually went out of their way to make gifts of their precious knowledge. Sure, I was being educated in professional wrestling. But I was also learning the power of politics. In 1973, when Bruno brought me into what was still called the World Wide Wrestling Federation, the WWWF, even the McMahons were nice to me.

Within months, I was "Rookie of the Year." The early '70s were very good times — it was like high school, but with money. Still, I don't think the McMahons knew what to do with me. All they knew for sure was they could not make Bruno look bad — so I had to look good.

I did some tag-teaming for a while with a couple of classics: Haystacks Calhoun (who should have been dead ten years earlier) and Andre the Giant (who I wish was not dead). A year or so later I wound up as one-half of the WWWF World Tag Team Champions with my partner Tony Garea. We made a pretty good team, and had some vicious battles with the like of Mr. Fuji and Professor Tanaka and the Valiant Brothers, managed by the infamous Captain Lou Albano.

Because of what I was able to achieve in the ring, life was exciting. And it certainly didn't hurt to be hanging out with Bruno and his cronies. I was always meeting some high-profile personality — like the time Frank Sinatra was in New York to record a live show at Madison Square Garden.

Jilly Rizzo was Sinatra's right-hand man and owned a local bar in the city. Rizzo was a big Bruno fan, so one night, off we went. Bruno, Dominic DeNucci, Tony Parisi, Angelo Savoldi and the token Pollock — me — were going to meet the "Chairman of the Board." Jilly's Bar was not a big place and it was packed. "Ol' Blue Eyes" was sitting at a table in the back meeting and greeting hundreds of people there to show respect. Henny Youngman, Shelly Winters and other stars were everywhere, so many that I can't remember them all. As I was standing among this mass of humanity, a rather small, skeletal old man slowly made his way over to me. In his hand he was holding a small cardboard tube — the kind in the center of a roll of toilet paper.

At one end of the tube there were matchsticks, secured with Scotch tape. He looked up at me and said, in a heavy Italian accent, "Do you knowa what thisa is?"

I replied, "No, I don't."

He answered, "Thisa is a Polish flashalight." Everyone was laughing.

Well, even then I was famous for my quick wit, so I blurted: "You know why Italians don't have freckles? They slide off their face."

No one laughed.

Out of the corner of my eye, I saw Bruno moving his thumb back and forth across his throat. He was giving me the universal sign for "Shut your stupid mouth, you idiot!" I had no clue why as the old man slowly shuffled away, clutching his cardboard prop. Later Bruno informed me the old guy's name was Carlo Gambino. . . .

I always wondered if the FBI got a good picture of me leaving Jilly's that night. Over the years I've more than amused myself with the fact that once upon a time I told the Godfather an Italian joke — and lived.

In the '70s professional wrestling wasn't like it is today. Back then, many different wrestling promotions thrived and coexisted in relative harmony. Because the territories were confined to small sections of the country, and because television was still local enough to feature programming from the immediate area, it made sense for wrestlers to travel to different parts of the country. If the fans kept seeing the same guys in their town, over and over again, things would get stale, boring — much like wrestling is today.

Around 1976, I flew into the Los Angeles territory, and that's where I first met a couple of other new, future stars: Roddy Piper and Chavo Guerrero, Sr. The territory was owned by the LaBelle family. Mike LaBelle ran the business end of things, and his brother "Judo" Gene LaBelle went from town to town to choke out fans with his famous sleeper hold. Their booker, a guy named Leo Garibaldi, came to me for help one day in San Diego. Apparently some guy was driving the promotion nuts, wanting to become a wrestler. For whatever reason, the gods of the squared circle had given this guy the thumbs-down. I was awarded the great honor: to act as guardian and protect the tradition of the "secret sect." So, when I said, "You want to be a wrestler? Get in the ring and let's see what you've got," what I — like so many before me — was really saying was "I hope you have insurance, kid." Anyway, I got in the ring to do my duty. Across from me stood a very big guy — this kid was probably 6′4″ and 300 pounds, not ripped, but a very solid, very big guy. I don't know what Leo was thinking; hell, I would have booked him. It just wasn't his lucky day — but he was way too big to mess with. As he came toward me his weight was all on his left leg, so I shot in low. I cupped my hand behind his heel and drove my shoulder in under his kneecap. His knee joint popping sounded like a .357 Magnum going off. He came about an inch or two off the canvas and fell like a mighty oak. As he laid there in utter misery holding his rapidly swelling knee, he thanked me for my time and thought he should go home now. One of Gene LaBelle's judo students came running over, yelling, "What a great move!"

I did not share the joy, however, even though the ghosts of Ed "Strangler" Lewis and George Hackenschmidt were smiling upon me. As time went on, I regretted it more and more. It really wasn't necessary. But that is how seriously the business protected itself back then.

For those of you with a strong sense of justice — don't fret. Just a few short weeks later, life would get one up on me once again.

It started one night after a match in Los Angeles. I received a message that some movie guy wanted to talk to me. I met him after the show and he said he was very impressed by the way I moved, for a big man. He was making his first movie, a three-week location shoot out in the desert. The next day I went to his office somewhere on Sunset Boulevard. He gave me a script and told me he would pay me $1,500 for three weeks and I would do my own stunts. I took the script home and did not think too much about the money. But after reading the garbage he'd given me, I didn't think I'd have done it for $1,500 per day (well, okay, maybe). The script called for me to run around the desert, fall from a couple cliffs and kill people with my psychotic "family" so we could eat their babies . . . . I did not have the heart to tell the guy his very first movie sucked. So I told him my wrestling schedule paid me a lot more money, and that I didn't have the time to disappear into the desert . . . .

Turns out the man's name was Wes Craven. He was making his first movie, and the film called *The Hills Have Eyes* was recently remade. The original — the film I turned down — became a cult classic, and so did Wes. I still kick myself for not taking that part. Maybe I could have had the chance to be Freddy Kruger . . . . But that's showbiz.

Fed up with Hollywood — just kidding — it was time for Bruno's protegé to hit the road and return to the WWWF. And hit the road I did.

I don't know why we're called professional wrestlers. We were actually professional drivers. That's what the life was all about. Driving eight hours a day to wrestle for ten minutes. Day after day, 50,000 miles per year, year after year.

After just three years, I felt I couldn't take it anymore. There had to be a better way.

CHAPTER THREE

UP, UP AND —
OH SHIT!

I was not the only wrestler who wished for a way to avoid all the driving, to just be at an arena and then magically get back home. It seemed like a simple enough wish and I found myself hoping science would invent some sort of nuclear-powered transmitting molecular reorganizer — but Captain

Kirk and Scotty were not going to show up in time to change the future.

So I did the next best thing: I started flying small planes. In 1975, I earned my private pilot's license, something I am still very proud of today.

The feeling of getting into a bird and soaring into the wild blue yonder, high above the rat race and traffic, with no cops hiding behind the clouds, was pure ecstasy — and the perfect cure for my highway blues. I almost felt sorry for the boys, those poor bastards sitting in their cars for hours and hours, paying tolls every five miles.

But soon I was feeling sorry for myself — all that flying around from town to town wasn't cheap, so I started recruiting passengers. I would be strutting around the locker room bragging about my wonderful flight and how it only took me an hour and fifteen minutes to make the trip. I knew the other guys had a five-hour drive. Talk about heat. I would go on to point out that I would be back home at 11:00 p.m., out at some club for a good time and dreaming about tomorrow morning's golf game hours before they made it back. It was a hell of a sales pitch, but some of the boys were just too scared to think about it. And some were just too damn big to get in the plane. Truthfully, most of the boys were pretty uptight about small planes.

In the fall of 1975 a plane crashed in the Carolina territory and the pilot was killed. Ric Flair broke his back and Johnny Valentine was paralyzed for life. As if that wasn't bad enough, not long before that Buddy Colt crashed his small plane into Tampa Bay. Buddy never wrestled again and Bobby Shane was killed. Even in light of these tragedies, there were always one or two brave souls who wanted to fly with me — which was all my plane could carry anyway. Gorilla Monsoon, who once wrote "You'll never make it!" on one of my ground school study books, was now eating his words, and a veteran private pilot, Killer Kowalski, was explaining to me that "flying was hours of pure boredom broken by seconds of excruciating terror."

The boys had a remedy to fight off boredom between towns and matches — it was called "the rib." I never ribbed anyone on the ground all that much because I did not want to deal with the revenge rib. Some ribs went back and forth for years. Up in the air passengers were at my mercy, and I do not know what mercy means.

But whether it was family members, friends or other wrestlers, I figured a few seconds of terror would always make their in-flight experience more memorable.

Usually a stall (the plane dropping down through the sky) was enough to get someone's heart pumping and me a quick death threat. My favorite scare tactic, however (which I only did when I was over some little, out-in-the-middle-of-nowhere airport), was to point out of the window to something that just wasn't there. When the passengers would look, I would lean out the fuel mixture. In a few seconds this would cause the propeller and the motor to come to a nice, quiet stop. I'd be shocked if some of the screams that came from the boys did not register on NASA's radar system. I think Tony Atlas holds the title for the loudest and longest scream fest. I nose-dived the plane, pretending we were crashing. This was actually a way to turn the propeller and restart the motor. Tony was crying like a baby, bellowing at the top of his lungs, "I'm gonna die! I'm gonna die!" When the engine kicked back in and I leveled out, he was so glad to be alive he forgot to kill me.

As amusing as those innocent little pranks were, this was not exactly the "terror" that Killer Kowalski had warned me about.

One hot and humid summer afternoon I was preparing to fly from Charlotte, North Carolina, to Charlottesville, Virginia. About a 300-mile trip. I'd developed a bad habit of ignoring omens of impending disaster and didn't pay much mind to a feeling I had when informed that the plane I usually flew, a 180-horsepower Piper Archer, was in for service and that the only other plane available was a 151-horsepower Warrior. This meant that with myself and two other wrestlers the plane would be at its maximum useful load. It was 95 degrees outside and so humid it created a foggy haze. To a pilot, this means that the air is so thin the propeller has nothing to cut through. It reduces your 151 horses to 1 hamster power, a tiny rodent running circles in its little wheel. These conditions are things to be aware of, but nothing of great concern.

My passengers met me at the hangar. Tiger Conway, Jr. was getting to be a decent copilot. He would fly quite a bit, either with me or Ronnie or Jimmy Garvin (they were also both private pilots). Our first-time guest passenger was one of the Puerto Rican boys from New York, Pete Sanchez. We hopped aboard and taxied to the runway. I requested the longest jet runway Charlotte had, taking no chances in the hot and humid conditions with a plane loaded to the max. Cleared for takeoff, I gave it full throttle and down the runway we went — kinda. The engine was roaring but the plane was rolling relatively slowly. I felt sorry for the propeller — I knew it was working hard at trying to find some molecule of air to grab onto. Not to worry, we were gaining air speed and starting to move pretty good. I needed the air speed indicator to reach 85 knots before the plane would leave the ground. We were at about 40 knots, with plenty of the runway left. At the end of the runway was an eight-foot-tall metal chain-link fence. Behind this fence there were always five or six cars parked, and people would hang out there, watching the planes take off and land.

With the air speed reading 70 knots, we still had enough runway left. Pete Sanchez was in the backseat behind me and Tiger. My copilot was calm and in control of changing the radio frequencies. As the air speed was approaching 85 knots, I eased back on the wheel to get airborne, but the damn plane did not lift at all. We were now rapidly running out of runway! I could read Tiger's mind through the wrinkles in his forehead. He was thinking, "Gee, in all the times I've flown with Larry we have never been this close to the end of the runway."

He was right. We were past the point of no return.

As we reached 90 knots the people watching the planes started scattering and running for their lives. Although I might have looked calm, my left leg started shaking as I pulled harder on the wheel.

When the bird finally left the tarmac we'd cleared the fence by maybe a foot or two. To this day I still do not know how I kept my calm; no look of worry even registered on my face. Tiger's face told a different story: "If I didn't know better, I could swear we almost got killed." Pete Sanchez in the backseat was completely oblivious.

The higher you go, the cooler the air. The plane ran great, the flight went smooth, we landed at Charlottesville on schedule. There was no doubt in my mind that the feeling of dread I had in the hangar was what made me request the longest runway. But I was wrong. The shaky takeoff was merely yet another omen.

The Charlottesville show went well. Tiger and Sanchez were both bragging to the boys how we made it in just under two hours. For most of the guys it was a six-and-a-half-hour drive through winding mountains. They were not looking forward to the drive back. I just wanted to get the hell out of there. There were scattered thunderstorms building throughout the area.

I loved flying at night. You had the sky to yourself. Scattered in the darkness and the lights of cities and towns. The winds were usually calm. On this night, however, the sky was angry.

We took off and headed due south. I was climbing as fast

as I could but there were mountains straight ahead. They were about 5,500 feet above sea level and I wanted to be above 8,500 feet. We quickly wound up in thick clouds, a place where a VFR (visual flight rules) pilot should not be. My co-pilot and Sanchez did not seem to mind. They were just happy at the thought of getting home early. Flying through clouds, you cannot see anything; at night it's complete blackness. As we were just about over the mountains, at 7,500 feet, the turbulence came out of nowhere. I thought the wings broke off at the first jolt. The wind gods had no mercy for that small aircraft, or us in it. They were throwing that plane upside down and sideways. One second the right wing would be straight. The next second it would point straight down. When the heavy rains started, the super-cooled drops sounded like machine gun bullets putting holes through an aluminum kite.

Needless to say, Tiger and Sanchez started to freak out. I was getting worried too, and we were bashed around like victims of a never-ending car wreck. I had full power and a full rate of climb, but we were descending at a rate of 500 feet per minute. I could not see and we were caught in a downdraft. A thunderstorm cell was building over the mountains and I'd just flown right into it. I was about to admit to Tiger and Sanchez that we could crash into the mountain at any time, when the lightning hit. Sanchez lost his mind. His bloodcurdling scream almost cracked the windshield. Tiger Conway, who was normally a black guy, turned white — with blue lips. He tried to calm Sanchez down so I could concentrate. He said, "Don't worry, Pete. If Larry panics, I'll grab the controls." Sanchez screamed back: "You touch anything and I'll kill you." Meanwhile, I was trying to fight the turbulence like I was avoiding a surface-to-air missile. We were dangerously close to the mountaintops, the plane was bouncing around, losing altitude, and the rain was pouring. Tiger looked like the living dead and Sanchez was in a trance, speaking in tongues.

I had two options: turn around and leave the area before the downdraft pushed us into the treetops, or try to make it over the mountains and hit an updraft. With my eyeballs glued to the instruments and after a brief, but sincere, conversation with God almighty, we hit the updraft. And up we went. The winds coming up the side of that mountain blew us up into the heavens like Dorothy's house in *The Wizard of Oz*.

We were at 10,000 feet and rising and I had no control. At 12,500 feet you run out of oxygen. I was not sure which was better to say to my loyal crew: we are going to suffocate in a few minutes; or don't be surprised if the motor stops and we crash. And then, Hallelujah! For some reason, God dug our little talk and we made it out of the raging thunderstorm cell. It seemed like a miracle. All of a sudden I could see the stars and the winds were calm. Tiger was getting a little darker, but Sanchez was still a vegetable. At least he was quiet. I was drenched in sweat. Killer Kowalski's "few seconds of terror" had lasted twenty unglorious minutes. It had seemed like an eternity. We landed safely at Charlotte and I finally stopped sweating. Tiger was black again and Pete Sanchez was on his hands and knees, kissing the ground like his head was an Uzi.

A couple of positive things came out of that original flight from hell. I realized I was stupid enough to fly into a thunderstorm and that I had the guts to look death in the face and spit in its eye. I was very proud of the fact I did not panic under pressure. I also became the greatest fairweather chickenshit pilot that ever lived. I never flew in bad weather again.

I was going to be needing all that self-confidence very soon back on Earth.

It was time to get serious about my career. And I felt a disturbance in the force.

CHAPTER FOUR

THE LAST OF THE RED-HOT ANGLES

In the late 1970s, business for the WWWF was not good. Bruno Sammartino, who recently had broken his neck in a match with Stan Hansen, had had enough. He left the ring and started doing color commentary. The championship belt, which Bruno turned into a holy relic, was now bouncing around between guys like Pedro Morales, Ivan Koloff and Billy Graham. But when the McMahons gave the belt to Bob Backlund, the territory really took a nose-dive. Nothing against poor old Bob — he was a nice guy and a dedicated athlete. But for him to follow in Bruno's footsteps was a joke. Backlund came off like Howdy Doody. In fact, that's what we all called him. Nobody could figure out why the McMahons made him champion. I always thought that after almost twenty years of Bruno running the top-level programming, which was himself, the McMahons wanted a "puppet champion" who would do whatever they wanted. It amazed me throughout the years when promoters would make decisions based on ego and power instead of what would draw the most money. They were giving the fans what they wanted themselves, not what people wanted to pay for. It still happens today. And fans still won't pay for a product they don't like.

The WWWF was close to financial collapse. The writing was on the wall: after six glorious years of keeping my mouth shut and my ears open, I knew it was time to make a move. I consumed every scrap of knowledge I could from the great workers, the smartest business minds and the slickest of the old school carny conmen. A game of human chess had begun. I thought I knew quite a bit: but I was about to learn I did not know diddly-squat.

I really could see, however, that the territory was dying. I knew only a big angle would revive it. And I knew the only man who could pull it off was the only man the fans really wanted to see — Bruno. Whoever was involved with him would be wrestling's next "super heel." I saw the light, and I called the man. I ran the idea past Bruno, about the student stabbing his mentor in the back to achieve his own identity. He said he would think about it and he did. I think the hardest part of the decision Bruno faced was that he understood his big comeback would mean big money. And big money would save the McMahons.

Bruno did not like the McMahons.

A week or so later I picked up the phone and it was Bruno: not only would he do it, he had the entire angle laid out. The way he was going to program it week to week made it a masterpiece. Still, we had no idea how huge it was about to become.

Bruno was going to talk to Vince Sr. and get back to me. Vince Jr. did not say much in those days, since it was mostly Vince Sr.'s show, and Vince Sr. was not all that smart in terms of angles or really drawing money. Like I said, Bruno did all that work on the top level. Vince Sr. would much rather blow his money on prizefighters or the racetrack. The smarter veterans would approach Vince Sr. and say something like, "Hey, Vince, remember a couple of weeks ago when you had that idea of me and so-and-so doing that thing in the Garden? I ran it by Monsoon, and Geno thought you had a great idea. I just was wondering if you still wanted to do it?" Vince Sr. would reply with something along the lines of, "I liked that idea the moment I thought of it. Do it next month."

McMahon did not like my idea. When Bruno told Vince

Sr. the plan, he didn't think that I would be a worthy opponent. I do not believe it was anything personal. He was just conditioned to believe that Bruno's opponents had to be 6′6″ and 300 pounds of ugly, brute force to draw money — and I clearly did not fit the clichéd bill. It really didn't matter anyway; everything at that point was now out of my hands completely. The fact that Vince Sr. did not believe in what Bruno had laid out added some rocket fuel to an existing fire. Bruno was already pissed off. It did not take long before the McMahons realized they'd made another stupid mistake. Combined with the fact that all the Bob Backlund fans were still dressed as empty seats, they knew they needed Bruno's services once again. And so did Bruno. When Vince Sr. came crawling back to say how much he now loved my idea, Bruno's reply was probably something like, "Vince, you told me you didn't believe in this. You insulted me. I do not want to deal with you." Vince Sr. wanted to set up a meeting with Bruno. But you need to remember how big of a star Bruno really was then, along with the fact that the McMahons were desperate. Bruno charged Vince Sr. $10,000 just to sit down and have a talk about getting in the ring. And Vince agreed. My career and future in the business, which for a couple of weeks I thought was over, was now back on track and moving full speed ahead.

The programming for the Sammartino versus Zbyszko feud was a work of art — an art that really has been lost.

A few weeks later, on television, it began. Bruno came to

the ring from the broadcast table to interview me after a match, but I walked right by him. Sammartino commented that I obviously did not get word of the scheduled interview. "We'll get him next week. Back to you, Vince."

The next week, Bruno once again came to the ring to interview his protegé. Once again I walked right by. Bruno looked confused. A week or so later, Vince Jr., who was doing the play-by-play with Bruno, headed me off at the pass and asked me why I would not talk to his partner. I proceeded to cut the most sincere babyface promo ever heard. I was practically in tears when I declared my undying respect for my hero and mentor and talked about how my career was getting lost in the shadow of his greatness. It was fantastic. The only way I could prove myself was for Bruno to come out of retirement and face me in a scientific wrestling match. That planted a seed in the minds of the fans, that maybe Bruno was ready to come out of retirement. The crowd was drooling for it, but Bruno said no. For a couple of weeks, anyway. Then finally he agreed, with the stipulation that he would release any deadly holds because he could never bring himself to hurt me. I swore the same and the match was set. Bruno was back in the ring next week on TV. The entire northeast went nuts and we went out of our way to drive them even crazier. We even had an official weigh-in the week before the television classic.

Honestly, I am a perfectionist. While the world was happy with a ten, I wanted an eleven. Back in 1979, you guarded pro wrestling secrets with your life and "kayfabe" still ruled. No one knew what we were up to.

So far, everything was perfect. It was now time for the match everyone had been waiting for. I entered the ring first, a little nervous. This was the big time. Suddenly, I went into what can only be described as shock. As the crowd was buzzing and all eyeballs were looking at the ring, I could not believe what I was seeing. A mortal sin was being committed before my very eyes: the finish involved Bruno being carried out on a stretcher, but some moron had left the stretcher in the dressing room. Any idiot would know it should have already been under the ring. What's the difference? The difference between success and failure. Anyway, right between the introductions, here they come. Two referees are carrying the stretcher out, in front of everybody. They shove it under the ring, purposely ignoring the crowd. And then I heard a guy in the front row say it, "Look! Someone's getting carried out on a stretcher!"

I wanted to die. I should have seen this as another omen. The fans were standing and screaming at the top of their lungs. Bruno was on his way to the ring! The match told the story perfectly. We started out very scientifically and then painted a vivid picture of the master outdoing his student. When Bruno got me in a hold, he would release it before I could escape. He saw it as deciding to not hurt me — I saw it as public humiliation.

My frustration became obvious to the television masses. When Bruno made a friendly gesture to help me back into the ring, I sucker-punched him so hard he fell like a mighty oak. The crowd was shocked. But they had not seen anything yet.

I threw someone from his ringside chair and brought it into the ring, something which was rarely seen in those days. They say the third time's the charm, and after three cracks to the head, I left Bruno laying like a dead man in the biggest pool of blood wrestling had ever witnessed. The fans were in a total stupor. Standing there silent, as if frozen in time. It was like that one-second flash when a nuclear bomb is detonated, just before the shock waves come and destroy everything in sight.

It took about a minute or so, but then the shock waves from that chair hit the fans right between the eyes. Every wrestling fan alive was seeing red. They wanted to kill me! I mean really, really kill me!

As they carried Bruno's lifeless, bloody body out on the stretcher (surprise!), my life changed forever. Even the Lone Ranger, Superman and Zorro were pissed off at me. I could no longer qualify as a hero: I was the most hated man alive. I got a call from the New York Police Department. "Don't go to Little Italy — there have been death threats."

I was hoping that Carlo Gambino did not remember the Italian joke I once made. In a period of about a month, I had three cars stoned by angry fans; but that was nothing compared to being overturned in a cab outside the Boston Garden or being stabbed in the ass. It was a miracle I made it to Madison Square Garden in one piece. But destiny was calling: it was the night of our big return match.

As I entered the ring as wrestling's most hated villain, the heat that filled the Garden was indescribable. It really was pure hatred. I always wished I could take the fans of today back in time so they could feel for themselves the pure emotional energy pro wrestling once produced. In one of his interviews, Bruno called me "the worst Judas of all Judases!" (That actually meant something back then.) The crowd wanted to crucify me too.

On the other side of the coin? Love. The fans loved Bruno. In fact, when Bruno bled, people dropped dead. One time at the Pittsburgh Civic Arena, when Ivan Koloff caused Bruno to bleed, there were four heart attacks in the crowd. It became a sick joke for a while. "Gee, Bruno, you got to quit bleeding, you're killing off our fans." I was wondering how many we'd lose tonight as Bruno made his way to the ring. Every nut and bolt that held the Garden together was vibrating.

In fact, the Garden was not big enough. They opened the Felt Forum below the Garden, which holds another five or six thousand people. They watched on a giant screen. Thousands more were turned away. When Bruno and I locked up, 27,000 or so people went ballistic. Believe it or not, all it took was one arm drag and the roof came off. It was a simple match — designed to unfold another chapter in the Bruno/Larry saga. In the end, after getting the heat on my mentor, Bruno made one of his famous, berserk, comebacks. I got stuck in the ropes, trying to flee, and Bruno was choking me like he was the Boston Strangler. He would not stop. The referee had no choice. He disqualified Bruno and raised my hand. My crucifixion would not have satisfied the fans after that, but it was the perfect setup for the next month's return grudge match. On television, I was bragging about how I beat Bruno with ease. Bruno's response was simple: forget wrestling, he was going to kill me. That's what the fans wanted to hear. Behind the scenes, the McMahons still could not understand how I could draw money. They were still trying to figure out how to keep Bruno happy and replace me with some 6′6″ 300 pounder. In the meantime, we were starting to have this match all over the East Coast, from Pittsburgh to Boston; Portland, Maine, to Washington, D.C. The ticket prices were raised, records were broken. "Sell out" was commonly heard and the WWWF started to print money.

They say time flies when you're having fun and they are not kidding. We were back at Madison Square Garden once again with a new attendance record and the fans were foaming at the mouth. We did not let them down. This match was different. Simple in design and another step up the storyboard. I attacked Bruno from behind at the beginning, but that only lasted a few seconds. He beat the hell out of me for just about the entire bout — throwing me pillar to post like the enraged gorilla he was. It was exactly what people wanted to see. But at the finish we hooked them. I simply left the building. Smack dab in the middle of my well-deserved beating, I ran for my life and disappeared from view. An eternity of my soul burning in hell would not satisfy the bloodlust of those who watched. But it was the perfect scenario to set up . . . a cage match. The place where evil could not escape the quick sword of justice. The McMahons seemed pretty happy that night. Not only were they back in the chips and bragging to all of the other promotions about the records they were breaking, they also found themselves their 6′ 6″, 300-pound monster — the man who would wrestle Bob Backlund for the championship the following month. The McMahons' big find was Ox Baker. A big man with a fearsome look. In the ring, however, Ox was the drizzling shits — and so was the match at the Garden. He was supposed to squash somebody so the fans would hate him and then somehow, next month, people would give a damn that he was going to wrestle Howdy Doody.

The Garden faithful farted so loud and so smelly on poor old Ox that even the McMahons knew they had to get out the hook. Ox was not seen again.

This left a vacancy for next month's championship match. Shea Stadium was still a few months away and this was the perfect opportunity to get more heat. I got plenty. Only it was with the McMahons.

I was raised in this business, along with the others from my era, with the idea that you became a professional wrestler for one reason — money. Forget living under the illusion that hard work, love of the business and talent were important. I was not exactly thrilled with the fact that Bruno and I were drawing the money but Backlund was making more than I was. My payoff something like $3,500 or so, while Backlund would get $6,000. It became the norm to pay the champion more over the years, but that was only because Bruno wore the belt and drew all that money. Backlund was simply not earning his keep.

I did not think I should make more, but I saw no unfairness in making the same. Bruno always made a little more, and rightly so.

Along with that, the fans did not want Backlund as the champion. It was simply stupid business. This began eating away at me. If I took the belt from Backlund the following month and was the heavyweight champion when Bruno and I were to have our big blow off, we would have made more money than the United States mint. If there was pay-per-view in those days, our buy rate would still be unbeaten. It was what the fans wanted to see. I knew Vince Sr. was still not convinced of big success at Shea, and even Bruno was not 100 percent confident we would sell out a stadium. It was unheard of at the time, but I would accept no less. I thought my latest idea was the *coup de grace.*

Bruno had no problem with the idea, but because it was my plan he felt it was time for me to learn to deal with the business end of professional wrestling. Bruno told me to call Vince Sr. and discuss the matter; I wanted to talk to him about my payoff anyway.

I probably rehearsed my sales pitch for a couple of hours before I made the call. I had all the bases covered and was pretty confident that McMahon might bite. I was thinking of giving him the old, "Hey, Vince, remember when you had this idea of me beating Backlund? Well, Bruno loves your idea. . . ." Well, I decided to be a professional. After one more rehearsal, I called "the old man." I was surprised when he answered the phone and, after a very polite "Hi, Vince. This is Larry calling," I started to present my case.

After two sentences, Vince broke in with, "Larry, what the hell are you talking about? Taking the belt from Backlund?" I respectfully replied, "But, Vince, everybody knows he's not over and I just thought maybe . . ." Vince cut in again. "Goddammit, Larry! I don't have time to talk about this nonsense. Let's just forget about everything!" Click. Well, I thought, there goes my career. It took a few seconds to realize that the biggest promotion in the business had just hung up on me. I had just turned twenty-seven. Pretty young to be considered a star. Promoters only cared about stars. After keeping my ears open and my mouth shut during my apprenticeship, the first time I opened it was a disaster. But once again, I did not panic under pressure. I called Bruno back and soon his words were burning my ears, "The son of a bitch said *what?* Here is what you are going to do." I went into mild shock as Bruno began carving out future events. All I ever wanted was to work. I guess I was still young and dumb but I was not going to let the hottest angle wrestling ever saw die before my very eyes. And so whatever Bruno said, we did. I was about to receive my Ph.D. in pro wrestling.

CHAPTER FIVE

CAUGHT IN THE CROSSFIRE

In the days before real contracts, the boys lived by the seat of their pants. There was only your word and two weeks' notice. With so many men of integrity in professional wrestling, it became a locker room joke after each promise to raise your right hand and say "wrestler's honor." The struggle between the wrestler wanting to be paid more and the promoter wanting to pay less has been going on since long before I ever got in the business and will continue until the end of the world. It's the nature of the beast.

I do not believe Vince Sr. meant I was fired when he said, "Let's just forget everything." But that's the way Bruno and I played the hand dealt us.

The next weekend, we had three secondary clubs running. Secondary clubs are smaller venues like high school gyms or an armory somewhere. I was in the main event, with opponents like Ivan Putski or Chief Jay Strongbow. The shows were already sold out — the boys and the agents were excited because they would make more money. The fans could not wait to see me get a well-deserved beating and I was, of course, a no-show! Not only did this have a negative effect on the shows in general, it sent a couple of agents, Gorilla Monsoon and Angelo Savoldi, in particular, into a panic. They were on the phone with the McMahons five minutes after the show ended. I had just made the first move in a game of human chess that put into motion the largest behind-the-scenes, no holds barred, tag team, "hold 'em up for money" grudge match the wrestling business had seen. It was Bruno and Larry versus a pair of Vinces. I would be more accurate to say that I was playing the dummy hand, while my mentor was the true master. In fact, just as Bruno had predicted, my telephone began ringing off the hook.

Angelo Savoldi was the first victim. He was responsible for some New Jersey towns, plus the markets around Boston and Portland, Maine. I always liked Savoldi, an old tag team wrestler. He was a nice guy. Mild mannered and no matter how good or bad the news was, he would always very calmly say, "Oh, boy." I found him quite amusing.

He was also a very smooth old school carny con man. When I picked up the phone, he said, "Hello, kid. We're all worried about you. Are you okay? You didn't show up for your shots this weekend. We thought you may be sick or hurt. Is everything okay?" I took the bait, of course. But Angelo was not reeling in the fish he expected. "I really appreciate the concern, Angelo. I never felt better and I'm sorry about your shows this weekend. But I had a conversation with Vince Sr. a few days ago and he fired me."

"Oh, boy," came Savoldi's response.

I knew his brain was working overtime searching for a reply. "Ah, ah, there's got to be a misunderstanding or something. I can't see Vince firing the hottest heel in the business. And, my God! Next week is the Boston Garden!" The Boston Garden was Angelo's big town. Angelo was going to make some calls and get back to me.

I said, "Thanks, Angelo. I appreciate that. I don't really know what to do." Being Polish, I could play dumb with the best of them and they would believe it. But the method behind this madness was anything but dumb. Angelo had good reason to be concerned about next week's Boston Garden show. Last weekend's small club no-shows were simply warning shots. The power behind the punch was in the upcoming weekend. Not only was the Boston Garden running, the Pittsburgh Civic Arena and the Philadelphia

Spectrum were also on fire. They were already sold out, with record houses. The main event, of course, was myself versus Bruno. The WWWF could not afford to have me no-show these major markets.

My phone was ringing again. This time it was victim number two, Gorilla Monsoon. I missed one of his shows and the next weekend he was running Pittsburgh and Philadelphia. He was doubly concerned. The Gorilla was a good guy — a very likable, fun-loving man who could not wait for the show to be over so he could host the all-night poker game (and relieve the boys of their nightly payoff). I liked Monsoon and it was with all due respect that I gave him the same bullshit I gave Savoldi.

"Vince Sr. fired me, I really don't know what to do."

"There's got to be some kind of mistake, Larry. I'll call Vince and get back to you."

I was sure he would. In the meantime, Bruno and I compared notes. Angelo and Gorilla had called him too, telling him I thought I had been fired and missed some shows. Bruno played them like a fiddle.

"I haven't talked to Larry in a while. You mean Vince fired him?"

We were driving the agents crazy and the shockwave had to be reaching the McMahons by now. The next day my phone began ringing bright and early.

The Gorilla was on the other end explaining to me that the strangest thing was happening. Nobody could find Vince Sr. Supposedly, he was somewhere on the New Jersey

Turnpike driving down to Florida and nobody could reach him. This was still a pretty good excuse in 1980 since there were no cellphones.

Angelo Savoldi also called that morning with the same story. How unusual it was, but nobody could reach Vince Sr. I knew the real purpose of their calls was to make me commit to showing up at their weekend sellouts. But I stuck to my guns, as well as Bruno's preordained script.

"I'd love to make the shows, but if I show up fired, I don't even know if I'll get paid. I just don't want any trouble. I just need to talk to the old man and straighten this out."

I should have won the Oscar for best actor in a dumb role. This was not the answer they wanted to hear. So after Monsoon swore he would get back to me and Savoldi promised the same with a sincere, "Oh, boy," I called Bruno. I explained the story of poor old Vince, hopelessly lost on a toll road, but he did not buy it.

"Nobody can find Vince, huh? Here's how we flush him out. When Monsoon and Savoldi call you back, tell them you'll make the shows because you don't want to hurt the business. But to protect yourself, you want ten percent of the gross ticket sales, in cash — before you wrestle."

This was starting to get nerve-wracking for a just-turned-twenty-seven-year-old protegé. But after picking my jaw up off the floor, I said okay. I wore a path in my carpet, nervously pacing back and forth, shaking my head as I realized that my childhood dream had become very real, very cutthroat, and very big business. There was no glory in it: no triumph of good over evil, no damsel in distress. There was only the money — and the fact that the show must always go on.

Bruno's crystal ball never failed. The agents' calls were right on cue. I told Monsoon that I would make the shots in Pittsburgh and Philly and what my terms were. Without batting an eye, he said "no problem." Frankly, I couldn't believe it. And then, after a couple of "Oh boys," Angelo Savoldi agreed to the same deal for the Boston Garden. I was amazed. But what an uplifting feeling of accomplishment — it's amazing what you can achieve from a position of power. Without it, you're just another job guy.

But power and glory do not come free of charge. Holding onto them is a constant battle. With our war of the wills ablaze and the failure of their agents to get me back cheap, the WWWF had no other choice. They had to call out their big guns.

On the carousel of life, I had grabbed the brass ring of power — it was time to pay the piper. He called me the next day, in the form of Vince McMahon, Jr. I didn't really expect this, but I wasn't too surprised. I am sure the McMahons were not jumping up and down for joy when they heard my demands for ten percent of the gross. Then, the following Monday at Madison Square Garden had also sold out — with a new dollar record. It was Bruno versus me in a return match. The last one before our big Shea Stadium blow off. Madison Square Garden was Vince Sr.'s town and where he made the biggest chunk of his money.

As far as he was concerned, there was no way I was getting a tenth of this show. I never really wanted ten percent of any show — I just wanted main event pay for being a main event guy. The feathers were flying and Vince Jr. gave it his best shot. I'll never forget his opening line, which was a very cheerful, "Hi, Larry, ha, ha, ha, haaaaa!"

Vince Jr. can deliver more "ha, ha, ha's" in one breath than anyone who ever lived. The boys loved to do locker room impersonations of other people in the business, and Junior was no exception. His laugh was always bellowed in an artificially deep voice: "Hi, pal. Ha, ha, ha, ha, ha . . ."

After the official greeting, he tried his damnedest, in a friendly, businesslike way, to convince me I was never fired. "So let's just get back to business and pretend last week never happened. Ha, ha, ha . . ."

It was not easy to resist. Vince Jr. had a strong presence of authority, even back then. But I stuck to my guns.

"Vince, I really appreciate the call, but your father seemed pretty cut and dry on the phone. I'd love to get back to business, I just need to talk to him first so I know everything is cool."

As we reached this stalemate, Vince Jr. did the most amazing turnabout in midstream that I've ever encountered. In the blink of an eye, he stooped to the lowest, most dastardly and diabolical form of sales pressure humankind has ever witnessed.

He started crying.

Like a baby.

"Jesus Christ, Larry. What are you trying to do, give my dad a heart attack? He's out on the turnpike and we can't reach him until Monday. You're killing my father, Larry. For the love of God!"

I just couldn't take the crying. He had me on the ropes. I almost confessed. I was on the verge of saying something like, "I'm sorry too, Vince. I don't want to be mean, I'm just doing what Bruno said so the angle happens and we all make lots of money." As I nearly caved to my moment of weakness, a godlike image of my mentor appeared before me. With stern conviction, Bruno's apparition pointed his finger at me and, with a voice as commanding as the almighty creator Himself, spoke these words of wisdom: "Do not be deceived. He's a promoter." And so I held my ground. I don't exactly remember how that call ended, but there weren't any more "ha, ha, ha's."

I didn't expect too many more phone calls from the WWWF.

CHAPTER SIX

THE TEN PERCENT SOLUTION

Telephone. Telegraph. Telewrestler.

It's amazing how fast news travels in the wrestling business. The weekend of the big shows had arrived. For the first, at the Pittsburgh Civic Arena, I did not know what to expect as I approached the rear entrance. There were already a thousand fans hanging around waiting to greet their favorites. And let me know how much they hated *me*. I had to cover my head with a suitcase as I dodged an onslaught of soda bottles and rocks. But getting in the building was the easy part. I still had to face the Gorilla.

Walking toward the dressing room, pausing to meet and greet the other wrestlers, I immediately noticed a change in their attitudes toward me. They'd all heard last week's behind-the-scenes headlines and my new reputation was carved in stone: it would survive the test of time and last throughout my entire career. To the promoters I was a prima donna. To the boys, from that day on, I was an inspiration. Although they would never say anything in public, they were elated that I was standing up to the McMahons. Even the young, frustrated heel Hulk Hogan cornered me in the locker room. At the time he was unhappy about being some big jerk that Andre the Giant squashed every night, and asked my advice.

I told him, "Terry, you're a very unique human being. You should do great in this business. But you have to get out of the WWWF and make a name for yourself in another territory. They're just killing you here."

"Thank you, brother. You're my hero."

I believe he took the advice to heart. He left soon after, and Verne Gagne made him into a babyface. Needless to say, he got over in a big way. Me? I was still trying to find out if "I" was over, or if "it" — as in my career — was over.

Gorilla Monsoon was supposed to give me a lot of cash upon my arrival, but I wasn't sure if I was going to get my money or Monsoon's infamous "big splash." The ticket sales for that night were over $80,000, which was huge in those days. The Gorilla was a classic character. He had a different opinion of money than most people. He loved to have fun with it, but would never sell his soul for it. Fortunately, it was an ideal we both shared. As I entered his temporary backroom office, he started his jelly belly chuckle as he pointed to my pile of cash. As only his sense of humor would have it, he'd figured it out to the penny. There was a stack of bills, and some quarters, dimes, nickels and pennies. Something like $8,263.67. I started laughing myself. The following night there was a repeat performance at the Spectrum, and Monsoon stayed true to form. There was another even larger pile of bills and coins, totaling maybe $9,127.43. It's always those pennies that crack me up.

On the other hand, I do not think the McMahons were all that amused. I was still having the occasional vision of Vince Jr., crying his eyes out over his poor old man (who by now must have had at least four coronaries and was hopelessly lost on the New Jersey Turnpike). But the show must go on, right? And the next night was the Boston Garden. And another ten percent.

I flew into Boston and took a cab to the Garden. The cabbie was a little old man who was about to have the thrill of his lifetime. The long, narrow driveway between the Boston Garden and an adjoining hotel was lined wall-to-wall with hundreds of wrestling fans. As the old guy turned in, I started pushing down all the door locks. He shot me a funny look, wondering what I was doing. I was about to tell him when some fan screamed it out for me, "It's Zbyszko! Let's kill him!"

A second later, the fans started bombarding the cab with rocks. Windows were being smashed in and the little old cabbie was screaming, totally freaked out. He hit the gas and took off. It was a miracle no one was injured. There was a long ramp that led up into the back of the Garden close by and, after making it through the driveway of doom, the cabbie had to make a big U-turn to get to it.

He made the U-turn alright, but misjudged the ramp. The cab got stuck. Two wheels were on the ramp while the other two were still on the ground. With the car leaning to one side, the Bruno supporters saw their chance to finish the job. They began kicking in what was left of the windows and pounding on the doors with rocks — and then a group of them got up on the ramp and turned the cab over.

We were now upside down, rolling around helplessly on the roof. The poor old guy was screaming almost as loud as Tony Atlas in my airplane. I was holding on to my suitcase for dear life (there was over $17,000 inside). They say that before death your life flashes in front of you. I had visions coming out of the woodwork. I saw my grandparents looking down at me, shaking their heads. Then my father's face popped in: "I told you not to be a wrestler."

I saw Bruno doing bench presses. My girlfriend was looking at my headstone, holding my suitcase alongside some new guy. At least Vince Jr. was still crying.

It was all over. This was it, my big finish. My destiny was not yet fulfilled. . . . And then, suddenly, we were saved. Humor me while I take a moment to thank some of the unsung heroes of any wrestling show: the security guys. They hustled me out and up the ramp into safety. I even think the old cabbie lived to drive another day. I think.

Angelo Savoldi was in charge and he greeted me with open arms — and a calm, "Oh, boy." We hustled off to his office and took care of business. He did not share the Gorilla's sense of humor. Angelo rounded off his ten percent to an even $8,100.00. No cents.

That was one of the most exciting and profitable weekends I ever had, but the excitement wasn't over, not by a long shot. Another earth-shattering miracle had occurred — they'd found Vince Sr.!

I cannot tell you how relieved I was to hear he had finally arrived safely in Florida — Junior could now stop bawling. I don't know if the McMahons saw the light or simply the weekend's gate (minus my ten percent, of course). But with the Madison Square Garden show coming up in six days, they'd had enough. The McMahons were waving the white flag.

Bruno's game plan had been flawless and I was getting the kind of education money can't buy. The next Friday, just a couple of days before the Garden show, I drove from my home in Parsippany, New Jersey, to New York City.

Vince Sr. wanted to have a meeting with me in his suite at the Waldorf-Astoria, a fancy-dan hotel in the Big Apple.

It was amazing how fast he got back from Florida. I took a deep breath before knocking on the door — I think it must be easier getting an audience with the Pope. Anyway, here goes nothing . . . .

Vince Jr. opened the door and a loud "ha, ha, ha" filled the room.

Senior was sitting at a big, expensive-looking table. He really was a smooth operator, a very dignified-looking older man who was, in fact, a genuine class act. And I guess, in terms of the wrestling business back then, he was the Pope. As I walked over, he got up and greeted me like I was a long-lost son.

The meeting we had went very well and it was unexpectedly cordial. I agreed to stop holding them up for ten percent and he agreed to pay me main event money. I will never forget how the discussion went, because it gives such insight into how the promoters of the day thought.

I said, "Vince, in my heart I see no unfairness in me getting the same money as Backlund — he's not the one selling any tickets."

His reply? "I know Bob is not over like we hoped he would be, but he is the champion and we always pay the champion more."

That's everything you need to know about the mentality of the old school promoters. What worked in the past is how things should be done in the present. They had absolutely no desire, or impetus, to change.

My response was quick and to the point: "But Vince,

Bob's not really the champ — he didn't beat anybody. You just gave him the belt — it's a prop; it's not real. The only reality in wrestling is who sells the tickets."

He could not argue with that. Actually, he didn't have any objection to the fact that I wanted five percent of the Shea Stadium ticket sales. At least that's what Bruno told me I wanted. A bigger payoff for me was no skin off Vince's ass. . . . He just paid the undercard guys less. I will never know the whole truth, but I know the whole program with me and Bruno was so hot, so big and lucrative, that either Vince Sr. just didn't want to mess it up or he was sharp enough to realize that Bruno and I were in cahoots and he faced a no-win situation.

In those days, like I've said, a handshake and your word were your contract; there was nothing on paper. Even though you had to go through hell and high water to get it, once Vince McMahon, Sr. gave you his word, he honored it. A deal was a deal. A handshake and some "ha, ha, ha's" later, everything was sealed in stone. I was in heaven. Shea Stadium was going to be a reality — and for good measure, Bruno had one more trick up his sleeve.

CHAPTER SEVEN

THE LIVING . . . WHAT?

After the McMahons and I came to our mutual agreement, I abandoned my quest for Backlund's championship belt. I was pretty confident that the Shea Stadium show was going to be the largest spectacle wrestling had ever seen. But Vince Sr. still did not share my belief. Even Bruno wasn't 100 percent sure. So my mentor reached into his vast bag of tricks and pulled out the straw that broke the camel's back.

The secret potion that enables professional wrestling to both survive and flourish has several absolutely essential ingredients. The most important of which, the thing that brings this fantasy to life, is the interview. How, and what, you say to the fans can drive them into a ticket-buying frenzy or keep them away in droves. Bruno was the unchallenged master at applying psychology to interviews. In fact, it only took one more to seal Shea Stadium's historic fate. Psychology-wise, Sammartino's interview was the best I'd ever heard. Don't forget, at this point Bruno had actually retired; he was primarily doing color commentary. But the WWWF fans did not want Bruno retired. And they could not care less about Bob Backlund, or anybody else for that matter; Sammartino, the consummate babyface, was their hero. They believed in Bruno. Period. What Bruno said in an interview was the gospel. As Shea Stadium got closer, the storyline was already too hot to handle — for me anyway. I got attacked by fans every night and Bruno did not make things any easier on me. He dangled the fans' biggest fear right in front of their faces. In a now classic interview about our upcoming cage match, after pointing out that there was no way for me to escape either his wrath or certain death, Bruno went into a frenzy. He was so intent on destroying the monster that he himself created, that if he failed, he would be so humiliated he swore he would never be seen in the wrestling world again. The fans went into shock. Never seeing Sammartino step into the ring again was their biggest fear. The psychology was very simple and very, very effective. Those words, so passionately delivered, guaranteed there would not be an empty seat in Shea Stadium, that thousands of people would be turned away.

Sure, I was learning from the master, but I was also a very good student. Bruno had taught me well the secrets of wrestling psychology and the art of interviews.

The secret of Bruno's success was believability. Even when I was a young fan, I heard over and over, "I know wrestling is a put-on — but Bruno's real!" That's ridiculous, when you think about it, but that's how credible Sammartino's look and character were. People wanted to believe him — so they did. The power of this believability is the most important thing I learned, and took, from my mentor. I twisted it around, of course, because I was the bad guy. I made sure people would say, "Well, I know wrestling is fake — but Zbyszko is a real asshole." And if there were a few who didn't already believe it, they soon would.

At the end of Bruno's wrestling career, about the time he started doing commentary work, he acquired a very unique title. No one's sure exactly where it came from, but it was probably either a local newspaper article or a wrestling magazine. At any rate, someone called him "wrestling's Living Legend." When I heard it for the first time, I got goosebumps. It was the perfect description of what I, like a lot of people, thought of Sammartino back then. In those days you never heard of anyone referred to as a living legend. The phrase simply did not exist. According to Webster's, the word "legend" can refer to lines on a map — or an old story which may or may not be true. But I thought the combination of those two words was a great way to describe a wrestling character. Ironically, Bruno really didn't care for it. In real life, he's the nicest, most honest, straight-shooting, humble man you could ever meet. He is extremely generous and comes from an old school morality and ethic. The believability of his character reflected how he really was: Bruno the wrestler was just as down-to-earth, moral and honest. He felt that calling himself the living legend was a form of bragging, like he was trying to put himself above everyone else. But even if he had no use for the nickname, I saw plenty of opportunity in it. It would prove to be the perfect vehicle to add more fuel to my heel fire.

Once Bruno fatefully promised the fans that if he did not destroy his evil, back-stabbing protegé, he would disappear forever, I could not wait until my next set of interviews. After bombarding the airways with my cocky attitude and disrespectful arrogance, I concluded with this powerful statement: "Shea Stadium is the last time you're ever going to see Bruno Sammartino, you morons. When I'm done with that old man in the cage, the wrestling world will fall on its knees and worship me! Larry Zbyszko! The new *Living Legend!*"

The heat? Indescribable.

And the audacity of it all. How dare I say that, or even hint at it? (I had applied the psychology I was taught perfectly.) I was way too young. I never did anything great. I was a back-stabbing liar. How could I possibly announce to the world that I was the new living legend?

Easy.

The answer, for the fans, was simple: I really was a jerk.

It did not take a brain surgeon to know that if I had the ring announcer introduce me as the new living legend I would get so much heat I would not have to do anything else. Working with me must have been like a night off. The hard part was trying to make it back to the dressing room in one piece.

One night in Albany, New York, I was wrestling Ivan Putski. A fan in the front row was heckling the hell out of him: "Hey Putski! You suck!" Putski ignored him.

Then he shouted: "Hey Putski! Your mother sucks!" And still Putski ignored him. But then the guy screamed, "Hey Putski! You're short!" Well, Ivan didn't ignore that. He shot out of the ring, ran up to the guy and started slapping the piss out of him. The crowd went nuts. Naturally, as Ivan climbed back into the ring, I kicked him in the face and pinned him 1, 2, 3.

I figured that would be a hot finish, but I misjudged the situation a bit. A damn riot broke out. Fans were diving into the ring, trying to hit me. A bunch of cops jumped into the fray and began hitting the fans with billy clubs. I was running around the squared circle, kicking and yelling like Bruce Lee just to keep people away from me. The cops cleared the ring. When I jumped to the floor, they surrounded me like a human barrier. We were trying to make our way through 5,000 boiling-mad upstate New Yorkers. About halfway to the dressing room, my barrier began to fall apart. A fan pushed his way through and punched me in the mouth. That pissed me off. I grabbed his shirt and as I was about to punch him, he dropped to his knees. I couldn't help it: I kicked him in the face and out he went. So what did Albany's finest do? The cops who were supposed to protect me grabbed this unconscious idiot and dragged him out of the building, beating him with slapjacks as they went. As they left me some guy kicked me in the ass, literally. I spun around but I couldn't tell who did it. There were too many people coming at me. I broke into my impersonation of George "The Animal" Steele and started running through the crowd like a gorilla gone berserk.

People will usually move out of your way if they think you have lost your mind. Some guy threw a chair at me. I ducked and it hit a lady in the head. There was an old guy who got trampled under chairs as a mass of humanity chased me to the dressing room. Somehow I made it back. Arnold Skaaland asked, "You alright, kid?" I said, "I'm okay, but some guy got a good kick in," as I reached back to rub my charley horse.

I felt something strange.

"What the hell is this?"

Out of my butt cheek I pulled the four-inch knife blade that had broken off when I spun around. That felt better. Someone had stabbed me! About an hour later I figured out a way to sneak out of town. I lay in the back seat while a girlfriend drove the car. As soon as she pulled out, the rocks and bottles started flying, denting the hell out of my Coupe deVille. I was yelling, "Go! Go!" So she took off. A couple of seconds later she stopped and they started stoning the car again.

She said, "Sorry. It's a red light."

"Forget the red light, you idiot! Go! Go!"

To make everything worse, I had to get a tetanus shot. I hate shots.

Apart from getting stabbed, this kind of thing became routine, occurring almost every night. I can't say it wasn't exciting bringing the new living legend character to life — but it did not come cheap. Over the years, I made a lot of payments — physically, emotionally and financially — but right then life was great. There I was, the new living legend, cruising down the highway in my almost new, dented-to-hell-with-cracked-windows Cadillac Coupe deVille. Stashed in the trunk was $27,000 in cash and sitting next to me was my extremely beautiful and psychotic girlfriend — who was spending every waking minute trying to figure out a way to get it. I could write an entire novel about this relationship alone, but no one would believe it. Instead, I have decided to inject the following chapter as words of wisdom to all the young, aspiring athletes and divas who feel becoming a wrestling superstar may be in their future . . . . (Good luck.)

CHAPTER EIGHT

LOVE

Love and the wrestling business do not mix. Period.
The end.

CHAPTER NINE

SHEA STADIUM

August 9, 1980. The day I'd been living for had finally arrived. I got to Shea Stadium early, about noon. The electricity was already in the air. You could almost hear it buzzing.

The locker room was already looking like the set of *Let's Make a Deal.* We had giants, midgets, Hulks, Japanese stars like Inoki and Baba, lady wrestlers and promoters from near and far. All were filled with the same anticipation and wonder. Could professional wrestling do what had never been done before? As I walked from the dugout to stare at 45,000 empty seats, I wondered too. I still felt very confident though. There were already several thousand fans wandering around the parking lot. My only real worry that day was the weather. I had nightmares about big thunderstorms and lightning striking the metal ring posts — on the pitcher's mound the squared circle was helplessly exposed. But the omens were all good. Neither mother nature nor the heavens themselves would dare interfere with wrestling history. It was shaping up to be a beautiful day.

I almost wore out a pair of wrestling boots pacing the locker rooms. My adrenaline was flowing, and I did everything possible to look as good as I could. I was pumped up, had a nice tan, and had luminized my hair so it would have a shiny, golden glow. Primped and perfect, I was ready for my well-deserved beating. Bruno arrived later that afternoon but we hardly spoke. He was in a different dressing room, surrounded by the many promoters who were busy kissing his ass. I was busy looking at my watch. The moment of truth was almost upon us. In a few minutes, they would open the doors — there were already reports about the parking lot being full. It was not long before they let the fans in and I couldn't take the suspense any longer. I paced my way back to the dugout to see for myself.

Oh, my God.

I could not believe it. In a little over an hour, Shea Stadium had filled up. Not one empty seat. More than 45,000 people had materialized out of thin air. The security guards were already talking about the thousands of pissed-off fans they'd turned away. I was in awe, and I wanted to run up to the McMahons and say, "I told you so, I told you so! So, ha, ha, ha, yourself!" But, dumbfounded, I couldn't make a move.

Never before had so many people who wanted to kill me gathered in one place. There and then, in that one precise, glorious moment in time, everything I had learned in the last seven years hit me like a ton of bricks. If you apply the right psychology to the right program with dynamic interviews, you can't miss. We drove these poor people crazy for months. They *had* to be there. They *had* to see what happened. If Bruno lost, they had to see his last match. Every New York news broadcast team, with its army of cameramen and interviewers, was staking out territory in the infield. There was even a movie production crew there, filming the cage match for a documentary. And yes, the weather was perfect. It had to be. God had a ringside seat.

When the opening matches were finally underway, I almost felt sorry for the other wrestlers. No matter how hard they worked their efforts were anticlimactic. The crowd was there for one match only — the main event. If there were nothing else on the card, it wouldn't have mattered. The whole thing was undeniable testimony to Bruno's star power, and even though I had played my part well, that night belonged to my teacher. Shea Stadium made Larry Zbyzsko a star, but Bruno Sammartino made Shea Stadium.

Pretty soon it was clear that the fans were getting restless. The closer it got to the main event, the more emotion spilled into the moonlit night.

The show built to its inevitable conclusion with the Hangman beating Rene Goulet; Ivan Putski defeating Johnny Rodz; Angel Marvilla upending Jose Estrada; Beverly Slade and Kandy Maloy beating Fabulous Moolah and Peggy Lee in a women's tag bout; Dominic DeNucci besting Baron Scicluna; Greg Gagne overcoming Rick McGraw; Pat Patterson pinning Tor Kamata; WWF Junior Heavyweight Champ Tatsumi Fujinami getting the three count on Chavo Guerrero, Sr.; WWF Martial Arts Champ Antonio Inoki beating Larry Sharpe via submission; Andre the Giant pinning an up-and-coming Hulk Hogan; Tony Atlas defeating WWF I-C Champ Ken Patera via countout; and finally, Bob Backlund and Pedro Morales beating the Wild Samoans to win the WWF Tag Title, when Backlund pinned Sika.

Now the fans only had twenty more minutes to wait. There was an intermission before our match, which gave the ring crew time to assemble the cage. As each section of the cage was set in place, more than 45,000 hearts beat harder and faster. Mine included. By the time the structure was complete, everyone's blood pressure was in the red zone. And when I emerged from the dugout, the Richter scale hit 10. The blast of air from 45,000 boos could have toppled the walls of Jericho, the Iron Curtain and the Great Wall of China. Simultaneously.

As I entered the cage I was so overwhelmed it was hard to act cocky. The news people were standing around ringside with their mouths hanging open, as if frozen by the electrical charge. But they had seen nothing yet. A few seconds later, from the opposite dugout, Bruno made his appearance.

The Richter scale shattered. The stadium crowd sent out a shockwave that almost sank Manhattan. There's only one way to describe it — a nuclear explosion. The cage I was standing in was shaking like King Kong was trying to break out of it. It was truly awesome.

As Bruno entered the steel structure, I attacked him. It was pointless, however, as he stopped me in my tracks. For the next five minutes he beat me pillar to post. He smashed me from one side of the ring to the other. Every one of the 45,000 people in attendance went ballistic. I had to come up with some kind of dynamic wrestling move to stop the onslaught — and then it came to me.

I hit Bruno in the balls.

That did it; the fans started running through the outfield trying to reach the cage. Police officers and security guards were tackling them. It looked like a football game had broken out.

Bruno was lying in the middle of the ring and I was jumping up and down, kicking him in the head. I looked up and saw a gigantic sign the fans made in the left field bleachers. In big letters it said, "We Want Blood!" We were trying, honestly — but Bruno could not find his gig. (A gig is a small piece of razor blade wrapped in a piece of tape — a wrestler uses it to cut himself, to get "colour.") Unfortunately, and painfully, it was lost somewhere in his tights.

All that head kicking was becoming redundant, and I could tell Bruno was getting frustrated fumbling around his crotch looking for a sharp foreign object. As soon as he found his gig and made it back to his feet, he was bleeding. I never did ask how many heart attacks there were in the crowd that night, but I did see men with white jackets running through the crowd. After we took the fans to the limit, it was my turn.

Bruno made his famous gorilla comeback and beat the hell out of me. After throwing me down from the top of the cage, he started smashing my head into the steel mesh. Blood began to stream down my face and 45,000 men and women were finally happy. As I staggered, half blind with my own blood, Bruno opened the cage door and stepped out into victory. With one final blast the crowd blew sky high. All was finally right with the world — until next week.

As I walked, defeated, back to the dugout, I turned to take one more look at a sight that will forever be etched in my mind. Shea Stadium is the greatest memory of my wrestling career — and the $25,000 payoff wasn't bad either. (That's twenty-five grand, even. No cents.)

CHAPTER TEN

THE AFTERMATH

As I drove away from the famous stadium, leaving 45,000 strong ecstatic, after putting the exclamation mark on the feud that made me famous, I believed there was a lot more money to be made in the WWWF. Why wouldn't there be, with all the heat I had?

But promoters do not forgive and forget. Bruno was hanging up the tights, again. I had matches scheduled with Pedro Morales and Bob Backlund around the territory in the major markets. As per my deal with the McMahons, we were going to do some three-shot programs. This was a good thing, because it meant another five or six months on top, making main event money, instead of living from show to show with a one-time deal.

Pedro and I were getting ready to have the first of our three matches at the Boston Garden. Boston had become one of my favorite towns; the fans there really, really hated me. It was so intense that when I wrestled they had to put up hockey Plexiglas, with netting on top, to keep the beer and whiskey bottles from reaching the ring. It was like wrestling in a birdcage. As Pedro and I were putting on the boots, the agent, Angelo Savoldi, made his way over.

"Hi, fellas. Say, I just got off the phone with Vince Sr. and he wants to do something a little different tonight."

I couldn't wait to hear this one. "What's that, Angelo?"

"He wants Pedro to grab a pinfall on you somehow."

Well, here we go again. What that meant in wrestling was there wasn't going to be a three-shot program, and thus no three main event payoffs. After you got pinned or beat clean in those days, the heat was gone and there was no reason to come back in a return match. This was a swerve job — a punishment — and definitely not what the McMahons and I had talked about. Unfortunately for

Angelo, I was already armed with a comeback that would stop him, any other agent, or even the McMahons, right in their tracks.

"I'm sorry, Angelo, but that wasn't the deal. Besides, Bruno never pinned me — this would make Bruno look bad."

"Oh, boy," he began. "You have a point there."

Making Bruno look bad was one of the last taboos in wrestling. As we worked out some sort of disqualification, I quickly realized my days in the WWWF were being cut short. It was time I took the same advice I gave Hulk Hogan.

So, the new living legend packed up his suitcase and hit the road. And what a long, winding and strange road it was.

Professional wrestling, like the rest of humanity, was about to change forever.

CHAPTER ELEVEN

REST IN PEACE

It was the early 1980s and the age of innocence was coming to an end. Howdy Doody and the Lone Ranger were transforming into the Terminator and Rambo. The supermen of the '60s like Steve Reeves and Charles Atlas looked anorexic compared to the Arnold Schwarzenegger and Lou Ferrigno of the dawning anabolic era. Bad guys became good guys —

and good guys became saps. The wrestling business had no choice; it too had to change with the times. The old school was on life-support and the golden days of the territories were numbered. Coast to coast, cable television was making the country a much smaller place.

Professional wrestling was about to become a phenomenon nationwide. And wrestlers had to undergo a complete metamorphosis if they wanted to survive constant national exposure. The simple but solid names of yesterday — champions like Bruno Sammartino, Verne Gagne, Lou Thesz, and Jack Brisco — were now metamorphosizing into surrealistic, larger-than-life characters. The responsibility of keeping the business thriving was placed on the broad shoulders of the Hulkster, the Macho Man, the Road Warriors, the Superfly, the Living Legend, the American Dream, and the Nature Boy — and the list went on and on.

Vince McMahon, Sr. passed away. The WWWF quickly became the WWF, with Junior at the helm. The verbal agreements his father and the other promoters had honored for years, respecting each other's territorial boundaries, were suddenly null and void. Some people would call the younger McMahon a back-stabbing so-and-so. Others would label him a true visionary. Whatever your perception, it doesn't really matter. If Vincent Kennedy McMahon didn't make his move, somebody else surely would have.

In business terms, it was a brilliant maneuver, pal. Ha, ha, ha.

With nothing legal and binding in writing, it was open

season on wrestling talent and on other promotions. You can use the words "stolen" or "recruited" — whichever you please. Whatever you want to call it, Vince McMahon's WWF acquired the top talent from the other territories. For the other promotions this was a huge and unexpected setback. Left and right, angles and storylines were killed. Hulk Hogan left the AWA, where the Gagnes had recently re-packaged him as a main event babyface hero. He was soon followed by Jesse "The Body" Ventura and later Bobby "The Brain" Heenan. The Junkyard Dog left Bill Watts' UWF and Roddy Piper headed north from Crockett's NWA. Other boys followed suit.

No doubt about it, these men were making a very sound business move. Now that the WWF had nationwide exposure, any market the promotion ran in the country would have a card that included their very own most loved or hated wrestling star. But it soon became clear that the other promoters were not going to take things lying down. The Crocketts, with their NWA, were on TBS, an ever-growing national cable channel. Verne Gagne's AWA had a slot on ESPN. The race for wrestling supremacy was on.

The WWF, with its short run on NBC, was already way out in front. Honestly, it was a historical milestone. Professional wrestling had moved out of the carnival tents to the ultimate in mass media achievement — prime time television.

In the process, wrestlers were becoming household names. Parents were tripping over the new plastic action figures of their kids' favorite grappler and more and more fans were coming out of the closet. In the eyes of modern-day culture it was now acceptable to be a fan of the mat game. The poor, stereotypical toothless yokel waving a rubber chicken was being replaced by a new generation of fans, both young and old, and richer and richer.

In the seats, the nearly homeless were now sitting next to doctors and lawyers and their kids, everyone chanting the name of their mutual hero in unison. And there surely was a pot of gold at the end of this nationwide rainbow. Good talent had no problem finding work; promoters needed new ideas and new stars. Superhuman characters like Sting, the Ultimate Warrior, Sid Vicious and Lex Luger were coming out of the woodwork.

CHAPTER TWELVE

SAYONARA TO THE OLD SCHOOL

The times were definitely changing. To keep up, wrestling was giving itself a facelift. I was trying to determine if there was anything I could do to enhance my look for the new decade, but it wasn't easy. If I bleached my hair, I would look like the current crop of heels who were still imitating Gorgeous George. If I acquired a fancy robe festooned with tiny gemstones, I would also look like the guys imitating Gorgeous George. I considered everything, from a handlebar moustache to becoming the "man with the golden boots." But none of these things were really me. I decided to put aside the ridiculous and see where mere talent and reputation could take me. The giant, muscled-up, steroid look was never an option — I was scared to death of needles.

While I was waiting for destiny to show me the way, I took a short break from the American wrestling scene. One of the perks of the business was the opportunity to see the world. Even better, you got paid to see it. One of wrestling's international hot spots was Japan. They loved (and still love) wrestling. I heard a lot of talk from the boys about how different it was wrestling in front of Japanese fans and I was excited about my first trip. It was a long flight from New York to Tokyo and I thought it would be pretty boring. But with a dozen wrestlers on the plane, how could I be that naive? One of the big names in those days was on the flight with us — Haystacks Calhoun. All 601 pounds of him. The Japanese had to buy two first-class seats just so Calhoun could sit. His ass was so huge it had its own congressman. It had to be five feet across. I felt sorry for Haystacks having to endure such a long flight since there was no way he could get into an airplane bathroom. I mean *no* way. This sparked the imagination of one mischievous passenger whom I will not name (Mr. Fuji). He emptied a bottle of liquid laxative into Calhoun's soda and the fun began. Halfway to Tokyo, poor Haystacks was dying by degrees from the inside out. He had to go so bad his horseshoe warped. While the group of us sensitive wrestlers were wiping tears from our eyes because we were laughing so hard, the flight attendants escorted Calhoun to the rear of the plane. As he was trying to squeeze that big caboose down the aisle, he was repeating like a Howitzer — farts so thunderous I thought we were flying through a cloudburst. The wrestlers, of course, were rolling in the aisles. They managed to get Calhoun to the back of the plane and pulled the privacy curtain closed. Like that would help. These petite Japanese stewardesses then held a big plastic bag under Calhoun's carriage. . . . And your imagination can take things from there.

The smell of the Haystacks' calamity reeked through coach and snaked its way to first class. Along the way, people with weak stomachs were barfing. By the time this cloud of doom reached the front of the plane no one was laughing — we were all ready to slaughter Fuji.

I could not wait to get to Japan. As I looked out the window I could see the massive city peeking through the clouds. Tokyo looked like ten New York Cities all lined up in a row. It was that huge. And like the journey over, there was a good chance we'd have an interesting landing.

When they built the new Nakita Airport outside Tokyo, the Japanese government took over a lot of farmland. The farmers, eager to show their political support, had taken to shooting at the incoming airliners with rifles and sending up small, homemade bombs by balloon. This was a comforting thought as the plane was making its final approach.

Japan was certainly a different culture, almost the opposite of America. We did a lot of traveling around the country by bus. The American guys and the mid-card Japanese wrestlers would usually gather at the back of the bus for poker games. I usually sat up front with Andre the Giant and played cribbage. I love playing poker but there were always ten or more of the boys watching the game who spoke Japanese. Guess who kept winning? I thought it was safer to sit up front. That is, until the day when the bus almost flipped over.

Some guy in a pickup truck pulled out from a side street directly in front of us. As our driver slammed on the brakes, the back seat poker game quickly moved to the front; the bus did a donut and Andre outscreamed everyone. The driver was yelling something in Japanese when all of a sudden the man in the pickup truck runs over to the driver's window. The culprit started bowing in repentance as our driver cursed him like a rented mule, and then — slapped him. Surprisingly, the other driver started bowing even more furiously than before. Our guy slapped him again. More bowing brought a third, hard slap in the face. The other guy genuflected again like he was thanking our driver for slapping the shit out of him. Then he got back in his truck and drove off. Can you imagine this happening in L.A. or New York? There would be a shootout.

The stories I heard about wrestling in Japan were true. Back home, the fans would scream and shout and sometimes riot, throwing beer bottles and other projectiles and generally having a great old time. The Japanese fans would just, well, sit. Even if you pulled out their hero's eyeball and stepped on it, they would sit quietly and politely applaud. I could never figure that out, or their sense of humor. If you gave somebody a low blow in the States, there would be hell to pay. In Japan they laughed their collective asses off. Trying to work a crowd in Japan was a truly unique experience. Most of the shows were in small towns out in the country. They would set up a ring in the middle of a field and then erect a ten-foot-high canvas fence around the perimeter. As a few thousand Japanese fans entered, they were given a sheet of newspaper. After a few steps, they would remove their shoes, walk to a spot close to the ring, put the newspaper on the grass and sit. There were no chairs. I still cannot figure out how they found their own footwear for the walk home: at times there were six thousand shoes lying around. Except for slight differences, intermissions were similar to those in the States. Half the crowd would get something to eat and the other half would go to relieve themselves. With no hot dogs or hamburgers on offer, the hungry would pick the most appetizing-looking squid-on-a-stick and walk around eating the dangling, suction-cupped tentacles. As you can imagine, I lost a bit of weight in Japan.

There were no restrooms at these shows. Half the crowd would walk over to the canvas fence and line up next to each other. There would be thousands of them, doing their individual things, men standing and women squatting. Then they would walk barefoot back to their newspaper and wait for the main event.

Yeah, this was certainly different than living in the suburbs. In time, I realized touring Japan usually followed the same six-week course. The first couple of weeks were a lot of fun with a great bunch of guys. The next couple of weeks, we all started to get homesick. The second-to-last week, fights would break out and we could not stand the sight of each other. The last week we were so happy to be headed home we were best friends again.

Back in America, however, a somewhat similar routine had begun to establish itself. The remaining territorial promotions were no longer on friendly terms. The move for nationwide supremacy had become intense and nasty. And on the way back from the Land of the Rising Sun, destiny seemed to be calling me to the Land of 1,000 Lakes — home of the American Wrestling Association.

CHAPTER THIRTEEN

THE AWA

I landed in the AWA around 1984. The exact dates of my wrestling past have become a bit blurry; it comes with the territory when you have as much past as I do. As far as I am concerned, the American Wrestling Association was the last of the great territorial promotions. The changing times and the rise of cable were relegating territories to the pages of history, just as supermarkets replaced mom-and-pop grocery stores. The AWA was not going away without a fight, however, and I was excited to be a part of the battle. In its heyday, the Minnesota-based AWA was one of the premier territories; it was difficult to get into and there was always a waiting list. Many of the business' biggest stars were developed there, guys like Jesse Ventura, Gene Okerlund, Bobby Heenan and Nick Bockwinkel. Even the babyface Hulk Hogan cut his teeth with Gagne. And then there was the younger generation, the game's newest stars: Curt Hennig, Rick Rude, the Road Warriors, Nord the Barbarian and Barry Darsow all came out of the Minnesota area. The head of the AWA was the legendary Verne Gagne, one of a handful of promoters who was actually a successful wrestler (and a tough one too). Verne wrestled in the Olympics and also played football for the Green Bay Packers. He was one of the last of the old school tough-guy promoters. I was truly looking forward to meeting him and other classic characters like Bockwinkel, Ray Stevens and Mad Dog Vachon. But I was also a little wary. Before my arrival, some lowlifes had walked into the AWA office and machine-gunned the wall over some dispute — I'm not kidding.

So, from the start I believed working in the AWA was going to be an adventure and after my first day in the office my premonitions were carved in stone. I distinctly remember driving up to the office building and getting out of the car. Jesus Christ, was it chilly! In fact, it was stupidly cold. My nose turned to frozen snot. I tried to spit it out, but it turned to rubberized ice before it hit the sidewalk and bounced back up at me like a rock. I was horrified. How anybody could live in that God-forsaken place by choice is still a mystery to me.

Anyway, I entered the AWA office walking tall and looking good. Good as I could with my hair all over the place frozen solid. I quickly learned that when it's 60 degrees below zero, no one cares about what they look like — they just want to be warm. Verne Gagne's secretary was an older woman named Mary Ellen. She was way too normal to be working in a wrestling office, sitting under a bunch of bullet holes. As she pointed the way to Verne's door she said that I "was expected." I came up with my plan: I'd do the "Here I am to save your business" entrance. After all, I was the "Living Legend"; I'd sold out Shea Stadium. But plans like that rarely work out in the wrestling business and my impressive entrance was hardly noticed. I had walked into the middle of impending intrigue. The AWA office had been bugged by the WWF! At least, that is what Verne believed. Shortly before I got there, some of the guys that the AWA were promoting — especially Hulk Hogan and Jesse Ventura — had defected to the WWF. Other strange coincidences had recently occurred: arenas Verne wanted to book for a show, for example, had just been taken by the WWF. Now convinced that the old days of loyalty were over, Verne was not going to tolerate the electronic surveillance of his office! Of course, no one hired an electronics expert. Why bother? Verne had Jack Lanza. A 6′4″ former wrestler with a handlebar mustache, at the time Lanza looked like Snidely Whiplash on steroids. That day he was standing on a desk with his head poking up through the ceiling tiles.

"I don't see anything up here, Verne," he said.

It wasn't easy keeping a straight face as I waited while Verne checked behind pictures of himself, or watched while Lanza climbed down and crawled under the desk on his back to look there. But I guess at this point in my career, nothing about the wrestling business surprised me. I could see their real frustration, as Jack shrugged his big shoulders and Verne scratched his bald head. When Lanza finally left the office, Verne and I had a very nice, productive business meeting and I was excited about getting to work. After shaking Verne's hand on my way out, I made it a point to stop and wish Mary Ellen a proper farewell when suddenly I heard Verne screaming.

"Son of a bitch!"

This was followed by some loud banging and crashing and then a telephone came flying out the door, bouncing off the wall by the bullet holes and breaking into a couple of hundred pieces as it hit the floor. A second later, Verne appeared, his head beet red, breathing hard, and looking like he just went two out of three falls with Crusher Lisowski. Pointing to the floor he yelled, "The Goddamn bug is on the phone!"

I stood there dumbfounded as Verne went berserk and Lanza reappeared in a panic. Little ol' Mary Ellen just got up and slowly picked up the telephone pieces, shaking her

The future "Living Legend" – from the black lagoon.

All dressed up for an exciting morning of church with little brother Terry and Mom, who you can tell loves getting her picture taken.

I'm glad Terry and Sharon were having fun.

With Grandpa and Grandma (gee, I'm glad I didn't inherit his hairline).

AT TOP: With brother Terry, who was growing up to be a hippie.
AT BOTTOM: The human game of chess: video games hadn't been invented yet.

Looking like James Bond for the senior prom: will the lady with the lucky number come and get me please?

Preparing to wrestle my destiny.

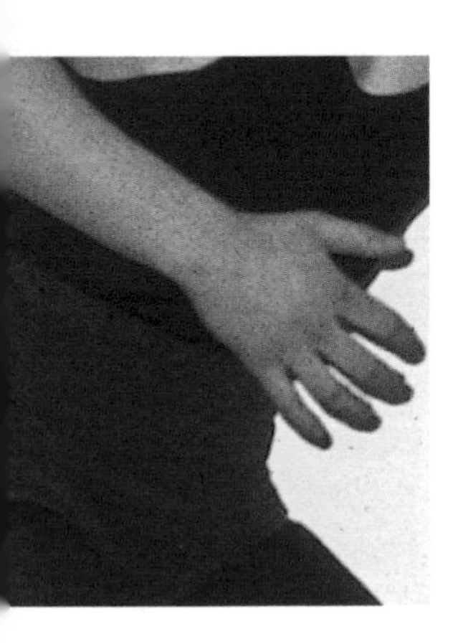

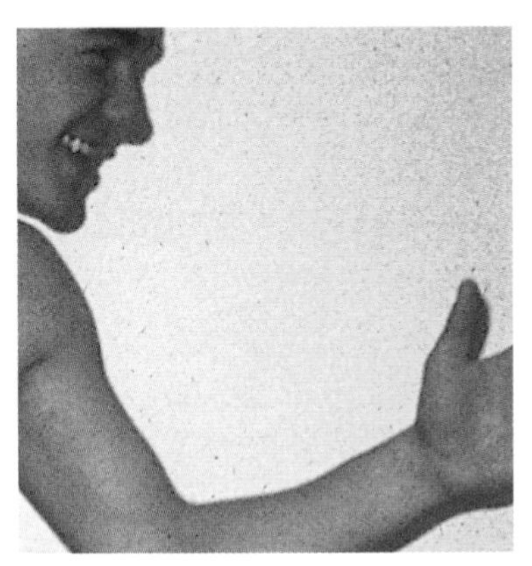

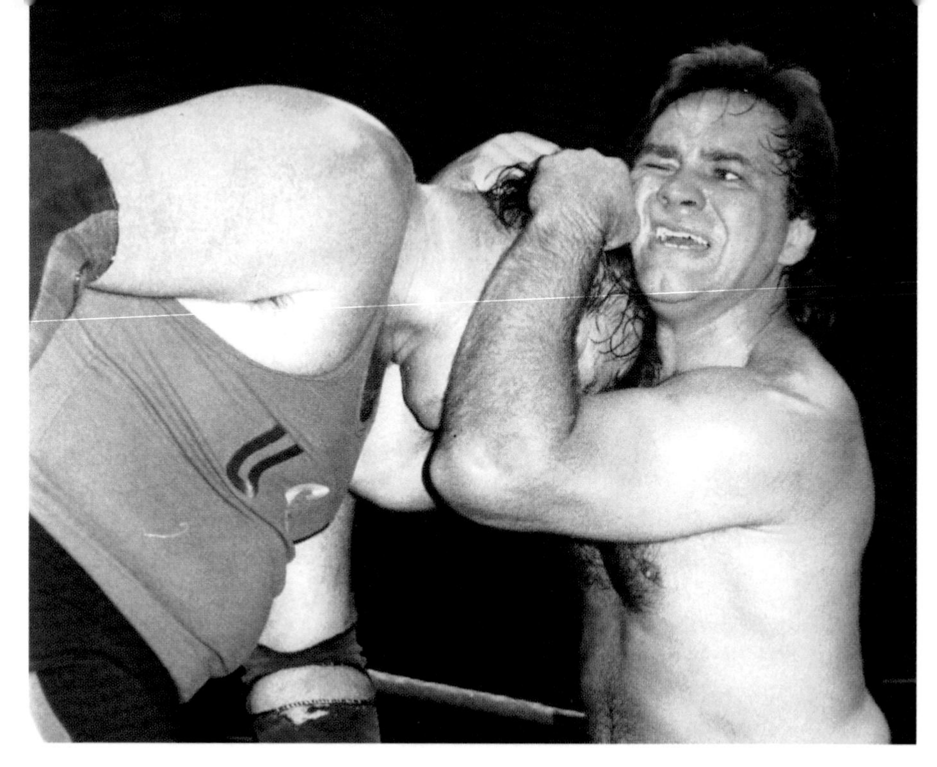

Trying to hook Sgt. Slaughter's head: his chin got in the way.

With my four tag-team partners – Haystacks Calhoun.

ABOVE: Hey ref, check his tights for a knife . . .

LEFT: Making a wish with Nick Bockwinkel's body.

BELOW: Choking out my ex-partner Tony Garea at Madison Square Garden.

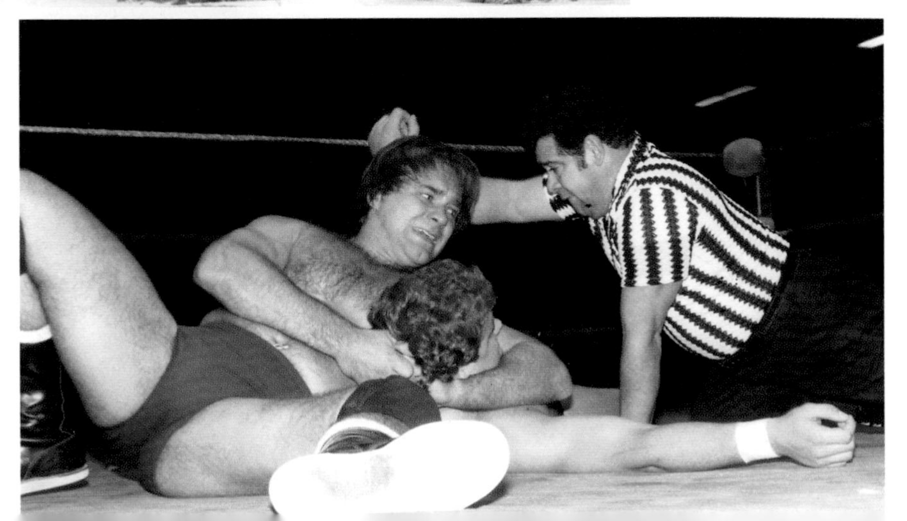

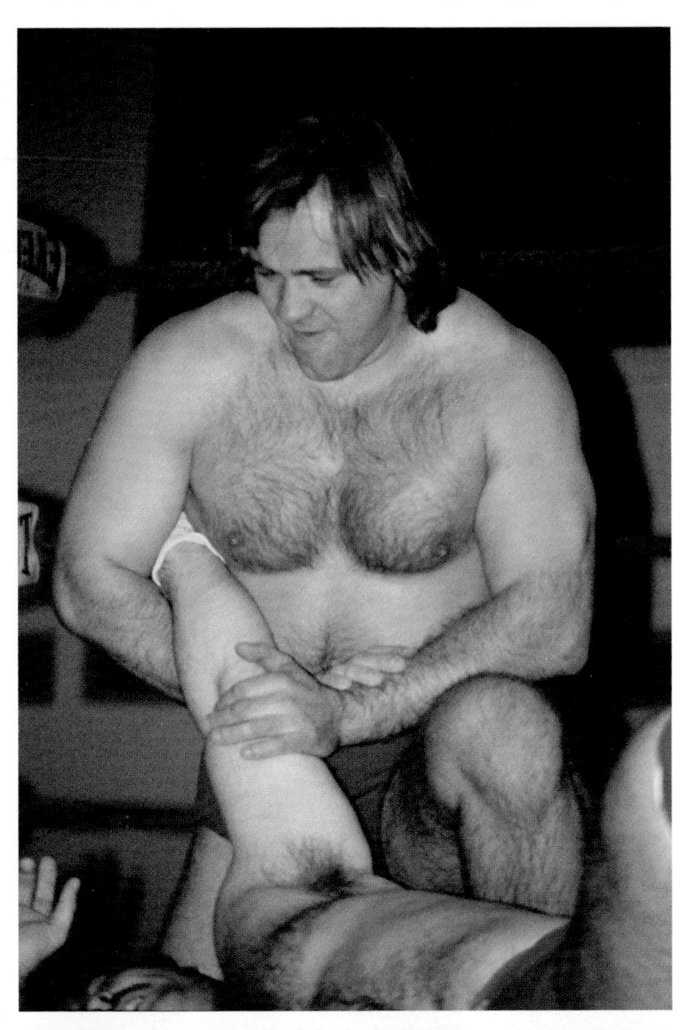

LEFT: Look Ma, no steroids.

BELOW: Practicing the armbar.

Bruno's friend Dominic DeNucci trying to get revenge for his gumba.

With Scott Hall: breaking in the next generation for the New World Order.

Sgt. Slaughter caught in my abdominal stretch: look at the size of his gut.

Just another day at the office.

Putting out the Wildfire.

Trying to make
Baron von Raschke even uglier.

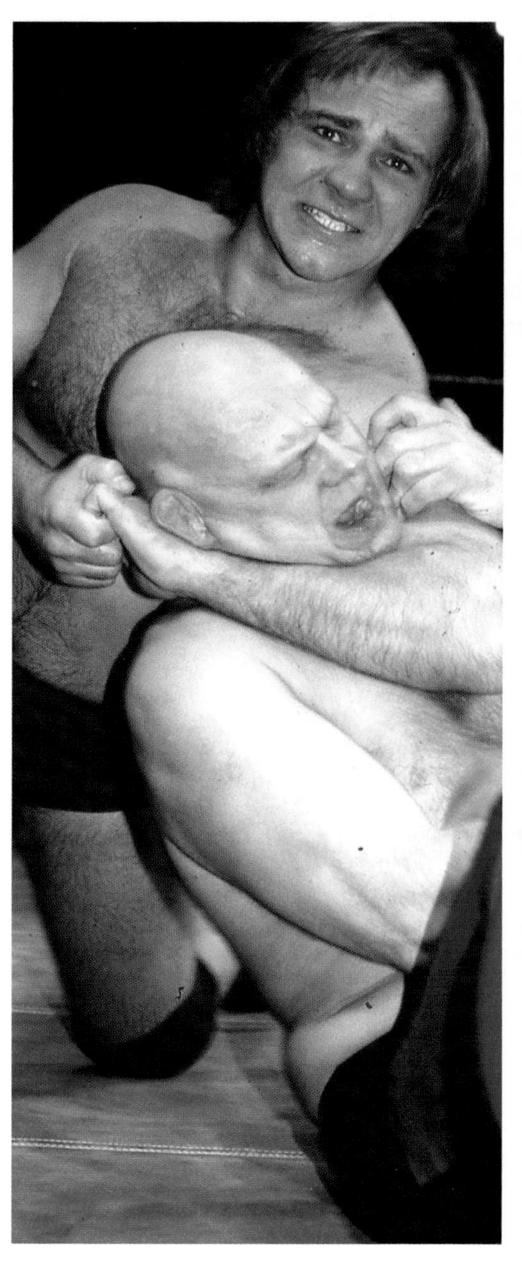

This is how the top
of Sting's head got flat.

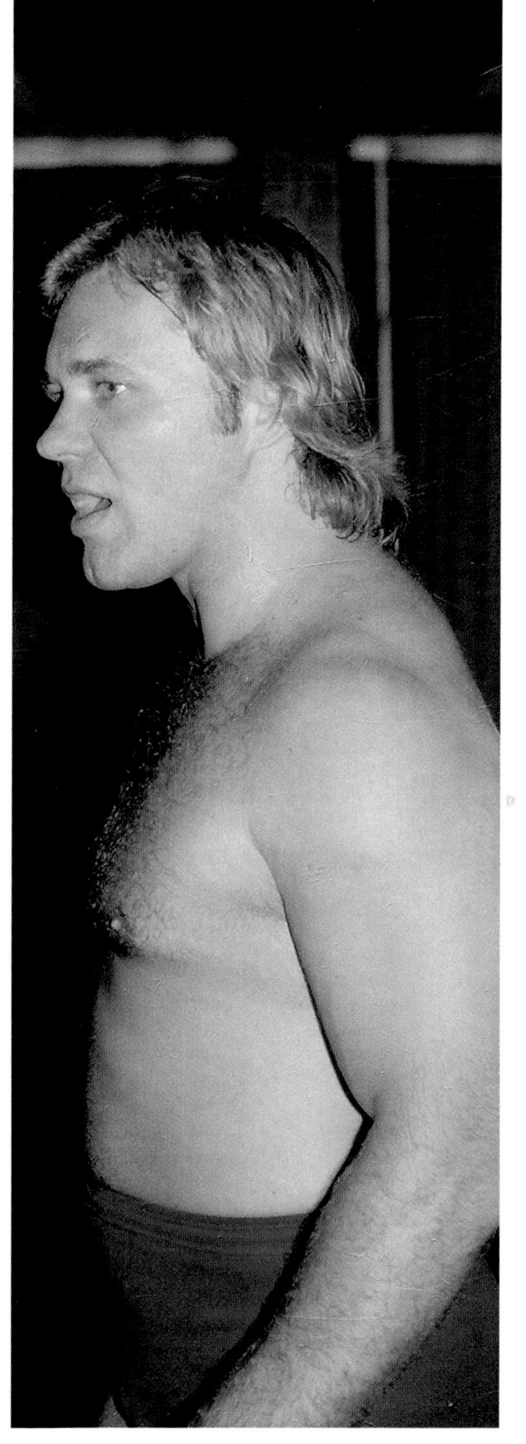

I never could keep my mouth shut.

OPPOSITE: With Mr. Saito and my Super Ninja – and eat your heart out Chuck Norris!

Beginning the glorious adventure . . .

And with the belt I defended up and down the east coast:
the Western States Heavyweight Championship.

head. Apparently she had purchased one of the new electronic gimmicks of the time: a small digital clock about the size of a quarter with a sticky back that people were sticking on dashboards, on typewriters, and yes, telephones. Very amusing, sure. However, there was a lesson to be learned. Verne was not as paranoid as he appeared.

A very short time after this incident, the leaks simply stopped.

Of course, Jack Lanza had just left the AWA and become an agent for another wrestling company . . . . You guessed it, the WWF.

The bug was right in front of Verne the whole time.

CHAPTER FOURTEEN

VIVA LAS VEGAS

Talk about the good old days.

If I could turn back the clock this is probably where I would go — with my reputation from the run with Bruno that culminated in Shea Stadium preceding me. My simple presence in an arena caused instant turmoil. All I had to do to drive thousands of fans crazy was, well, just stand there.

The phenomenon was so remarkable that critics would write about it and honor me as inventing the art of "stalling," although really it was nothing but good old-fashioned "heat." Doing my job and making money was so easy and fun I should have felt guilty. What the everyday person would have called their daily grind, for me, was more like high school with money. And it was only going to get better, for one of the most important things to a wrestler was television exposure — and the AWA was going nationwide on ESPN. If that wasn't exciting enough, every three weeks we taped the shows in Las Vegas. Those really were the glory days that Bruce Springsteen would sing about. Except for Nick Bockwinkel, every three weeks, for a couple of days, nobody even considered sleeping. Somehow, between the parties and the poker, we found time to put on wrestling matches and develop some new talent. The AWA did a great job when it came to creating characters, whether it was the young kids, like the team we called the Midnight Rockers (which propelled Shawn Michaels to superstardom), or the veteran who became one of my favorites as the infamous Colonel DeBeers.

DeBeers is a perfect example of how current affairs influence pro wrestling. In the mid 1980s when the prejudice of South African politics was daily news, an "heir" to the famous De Beers Diamond Mines (and, of course, the greatest wrestler in the world) appeared in the AWA with a hatred of anyone who had a tan darker than George Hamilton. This led, ultimately, to a great feud with Jimmy "Superfly" Snuka. But my favorite DeBeers classic was a match with the late Kerry Von Erich. It happened one night at the Showboat, when we were taping for ESPN. Von Erich had been in a horrific motorcycle accident sometime before and had lost a foot. With the aid of a specially made boot, he could get in the ring and work like anyone else and you would never know. (And truly, nobody at this time knew anything.) It was one of the best-kept secrets in wrestling. So well kept that Colonel DeBeers didn't know either. I was watching the match from the dressing room when DeBeers, who at the time had great heat, had the place going nuts. During his aggressive onslaught in the ring he had Von Erich back down on the mat. Poor Kerry seemed almost helpless when the evil Colonel grabbed his leg. DeBeers stood over Von Erich's prone body, about to apply a painful ankle lock; then when he went to twist Kerry's boot, off it came — literally — with an almost audible "POP!" For a few seconds, it seemed that time had stopped. Von Erich was lying there in the middle of the ring with his leg sticking up in the air. It just seemed to come to a point, with absolutely nothing where the foot should have been. The crowd was frozen silent, and the Colonel freaked out. Thinking that somehow he'd pulled off Von Erich's actual foot, he let out a scream and tossed the boot into the air like a hot potato.

I am going to pause here a minute and ask you, the reader, this simple question: if you were Kerry Von Erich what would you do in this moment of panic, in front of a live crowd and television cameras?

Tic-toc, tic-toc, tic-toc. Time's up.

Here's what happened: in front of a still-disbelieving,

dead-quiet and shocked crowd, Von Erich scrambled to his boot, grabbed it and rolled out to the floor, almost landing in the lap of a much younger Professor Mike Tenay. Von Erich then disappeared under the ring. And he was there for a few minutes, which seems like an eternity when you are filming a match. Then, lo and behold, a miracle. Kerry came flying back into the ring like he just ate Popeye's can of spinach, and finished the match with a completely befuddled Colonel DeBeers. To my amazement the crowd got back into it, like they couldn't believe what they just saw really had happened.

It may have been one of the last times I ever saw fans completely carried away by the spectacle. So many people by that time were bending over backwards to expose the wrestling business and its past secrets that some people had actually started to make a living off the enterprise. A part of the audience was starting to show up not for the matches, but to look for mistakes so they could yell "you screwed up" (or worse) or "boring." The true art of becoming a top-notch pro wrestler was becoming lost. The new breed of educated or "smart" fans was becoming frustrating to a younger generation of talent who looked great, but didn't know what to do in the ring. I looked at this change in fan mentality as a challenge and discovered an interesting loophole that had been created by the rise of nationwide cable TV. I used these ingredients to create something new in pro wrestling, something the fans had never heard or seen before.

CHAPTER FIFTEEN

THANK GOD — I SUCK

The truth was the fans were now arriving at arenas to be part of the show instead of just watching it. A decade earlier you'd see a hundred people evacuate ringside, leaving old people trampled under chairs, simply because the bad guy had jumped to the floor. Today's fans would stand there and laugh; children and old ladies alike would flip you the finger.

Digging down deep into my veteran bag of tricks, I pulled out one of my prized possessions. It was simply knowledge, the thing that made all the past greats, great. Knowledge, more than anything else, teaches you how to add realism to your character. Bruno looked like he could squeeze the life out of you with a bear hug. Chief Jay Strongbow looked more like an Indian than Geronimo, and he was Italian. Who did not believe George Steele was an animal? Everything I did, from the way I walked, gave interviews, wrestled, or even just stood, was designed to piss people off. It did not matter if anybody believed pro wrestling was real, they believed I was a real asshole — in the ring and in real life. With this planted in their brains, plus the fact they all wanted to be part of the show, I pied-pipered them to break through the barrier of network censorship and take advantage of TV's new, slightly more liberal parameters. You see, I got crowds to start chanting "Larry sucks." Sure, that doesn't sound like much now, when every other word begins with an "F." But back then it was earth-shattering. Hell, it would be years before you could say, "I'm gonna kick your ass" on air. It happened at a TV taping, when I was walking to the ring and I saw two guys wearing hats that read "Larry sucks." Of course, being a wise veteran, I immediately stole their idea. I had worked out a deal with our announcer, Larry Nelson. Every time I turned my back to him in Vegas Larry would move his arms up and down and incite the crowd to chant. Then, when I turned around all pissed off, he would stand there like nothing happened. We'd do it again and the crowd would chant louder.

After a couple weeks the routine became a phenomenon set in stone. Once it hit national television, it was smooth sailing. The fans now had an easy way to become part of any show with me. Every arena I went to, even overseas, fans would chant "Larry sucks" by the thousands and I, like them, loved it. I milked that chant for twenty years. You can imagine how proud my parents were. "Yeah, everybody thinks he's an asshole and says he sucks. . . ."

And how proud was I? Even an asshole has to be ready to bend with the wind. The secret of success, of course, was longevity, to keep going as long as possible. And you always had to be ready to add a new dimension to your character so the fans wouldn't tire of seeing you. I was still doing everything I could to make my wrestling dreams come true. I truly believed it was my destiny to be one of the great heavyweight champions of the world. And though it's not easily obtained and you need real talent, it's still more luck and timing than anything else.

As usual, fate was dealing a different hand than the one I wanted to play. While the old school mentality that was ingrained in me wanted the new "Living Legend," the man who retired his famous mentor at a historical showdown, to stand tall wearing the holy grail of pro wrestling — the World Heavyweight Championship title — the powers that be had other ideas.

CHAPTER SIXTEEN

PARDON MY COCONUT

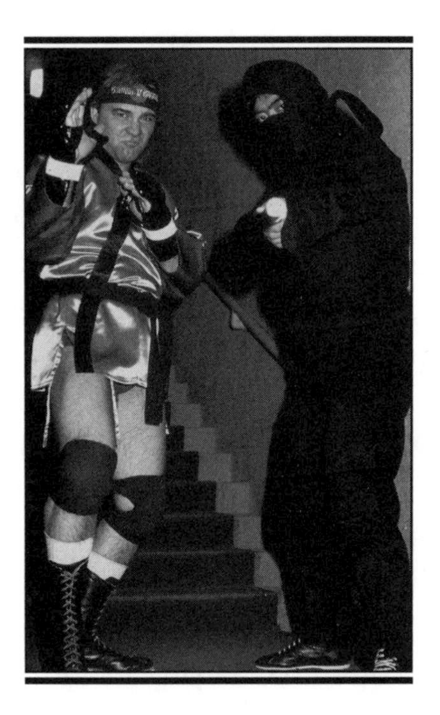

Years earlier, when I wrestled as an amateur in high school and college, I used to take karate lessons between seasons. I figured this would keep my reflexes sharp and improve my balance so I could make quick movements. I was never very serious about the philosophical martial arts stuff. I knew, one-on-one, a good submission wrestler could beat anybody. If there's more than one guy, your best bet is to just to shoot on them. The style I took was an Okinawan form, called Isshinryu. It was a strong, direct style compared to something like tae kwan do, which is more like a violent ballet. But I enjoyed it and it served its purpose. I never made it to black belt, which involved mastering weapons called a bow and sys. The bow is a long stick, while the sys look like a couple of daggers. I did, however, enjoy playing around with nunchuks. They were easy to carry around and I got pretty good with 'em. I liked to swing them around before a match to loosen up and keep myself sharp. One fateful day before a show, I was in the shower room, swinging the nunchuks, warming up, laughing to myself about the time Ole Anderson tried them and almost knocked himself out. I was going pretty good until I almost knocked myself out too. A loud scream scared the crap out of me. It was Verne, standing in the doorway.

"What in the hell are those?" I explained to him that it was a deadly martial arts weapon and he yelled again, "That's the kind of shit I'm talking about!" Then he simply took off down the hallway like he'd just seen Santa Claus.

Promoters were always looking for something new, especially now that they were competing for nationwide notoriety. The next thing I knew I was walking around in shiny karate jackets and ninjas were coming out of the woodwork. It all felt a bit strange at first, but I decided that in the best interest of my career it was a good idea to add another dimension to my character and in a way it all made sense. Of course, the new living legend of wrestling had also mastered the martial arts; of course I'd had my hands registered as lethal weapons. If I should ever be in jeopardy of losing a match, I would always come out victorious by bravely hiding behind my ninja or knocking someone out with my deadly nunchuks. They were, after all, a pretty handy weapon and they'd definitely clear a path through irate fans when I needed to escape an arena.

I think the most old-fashioned guy in wrestling was good old Verne. I remember one interview day, in particular, which became a classic. My new persona had developed and it was time to demonstrate how nasty the nunchuks really could be. Armed with my imagination and a bag full of coconuts, I proudly made my way to the set. With a little help from one of our producers, a guy known as "Polish Joe," we set up a little stand and placed a coconut on it — like we were teeing up a golf ball four feet in the air. After a minute or two of talking about how great I was, I would shatter the coconut with the nunchuks so everybody could see what was going to happen to Nick Bockwinkel's head. Shatter isn't the right word, actually; the damned coconut exploded like a hand grenade. Verne loved it and I was pretty impressed myself. These things could smash your head in and Bockwinkel was understandably horrified. In fact, the coconut shattered so fast the camera couldn't get it on tape. We had to shoot the demolition four or five times, each time a little slower.

We were in Atlantic City, New Jersey, when I finally turned

on Bockwinkel and knocked him out with the nunchuks, but I actually had to hold them together when I hit him. There was no way to swing them properly and make it look good without potatoing (truly hurting) poor Nick. And even when that didn't work, everything was okay because if the nunchuks didn't get you, the Ninja would.

There were actually three ninjas. The first of the deadly trio was direct from Japan, Mr. Go. He was a nice guy, but he didn't speak much English, so we didn't have a lot to say to each other. After a couple months, for some reason I can't remember, Mr. Go got up and went. But for my karate kid gig, the ninja thing had a good look. Verne wasted no time importing another Japanese wrestler — this time it was a twenty-two-year-old, 6′5″, 280 pounder named Howard.

Howard was so big for a Japanese kid we called him the Super Ninja. Howard thought this was the greatest thing since sake. He was a real nice young guy and I felt like a babysitter more than a partner, but I helped him out as much as I could. I even helped him out when he got a crush on one of my friends, the late great lady wrestler and valet, Sherri Martel. After I fixed him up with her, the poor kid went from 280 to about 230 pounds in a couple of months. I don't know if Howard got scared or just freaked out after losing so much weight, but it wasn't long before Howard followed in the footsteps of Mr. Go and was gone.

Verne still liked the ninja gimmick, but he wisely stopped importing them. So now we had a homegrown ninja — Steve Olsonowski. Imagine that, a Polish ninja.

Steve was a good friend and we hung out a lot in those AWA days. He would act as my copilot when we flew off to do house shows. There's a scary thought, two Pollocks flying together — I only scared the crap out of him a couple times. We also used to play a lot of golf together. Steve and I were righties. We often played with Jesse Ventura and an ex–baseball player named Paul Seibert who were both lefties. It was the classic golf battle. It was a great time and when Jesse became governor he was going to name the island hole at Edinburgh Larryland. But when my mighty ninja Steve married Paul's girlfriend, well, that took care of the foursome.

But we did manage to pull off a classic wrestling matchup in 1986. It was a wrestler/karate killer versus an ex–boxer at WrestleRock. For some reason I still do not understand, for a long while promoters were convinced that wrestling and rock and roll went together like peas and carrots. The shows I've seen that featured the pairing always lost half the crowd by the time the band started playing. It wasn't that bad at WrestleRock, but Verne had trouble with some rock and roll band — and wound up with Waylon Jennings. That's Verne.

A few months before this event Gagne brought in a former prizefighter who lived in Minneapolis named Scott LeDoux (according to him, he should have beaten Ali, but somehow he didn't . . .) to be a "troubleshooting" referee. Scott did a pretty good job and the fans bought him as a take-no-crap kinda guy. It was the perfect scenario for a buildup to a novelty match. Even though Scott was easygoing, I got the feeling that after two months of me calling him "Canvas Back" and "One Shot LeDoux," he'd really love to punch me in the mouth. The funniest thing about this whole confrontation was Olsonowski trying to be a ninja and doing karate moves. Man, he sucked. But he sucked so bad it was great, in an entertaining sort of way. For the AWA, WrestleRock was a pretty successful event, even though I still believe it would have drawn the same amount of people without Waylon Jennings.

As I made my way to the ring accompanied by my Ninja of Death (Mr. O.), I could once more feel electricity in the crowd. They hated me, and this was going to be great. The crowd popped when Scott made his entrance. The fans wanted to see me get punched out so badly they could taste it. We made the match a big production — even the referee was a famous local, a kick-ass retired wrestler, Larry "the Ax" Henning. When the bell rang the crowd exploded. The noise was intense, which really is rare in an outdoor stadium. I have to say, Scott came through and did a great job. We put on what is probably the best wrestler versus boxer match you will ever see. (They're usually terrible.) Of course, in the end he gave me the "punch heard around the world." Down I went and the fans were elated. It must have been my lucky day, however — I was saved by the bell. When I saw the replay of Scott's big right hand, it looked like my head exploded as sweat shattered through the air. I was surprised because I didn't feel a thing. I always wondered if I would have made a good boxer, but I just didn't like the idea of getting punched in the face. When I got back to the dressing room some of the boys were applauding, and Harley Race paid me one of the biggest compliments I would ever get. He said, "That had to be a shoot, nobody can work that good."

Thanks Harley.

CHAPTER SEVENTEEN

THE WORLD'S GREATEST ADVICE

Shortly after WrestleRock, my ninjas vanished back into the woodwork from which they came. The shiny karate outfits and my deadly nunchuks found their way into a box in the attic. I was, however, still feuding with the champ, Nick Bockwinkel, and there was further change in the wind. Nick was getting ready to transition into retirement and the AWA championship would be up for grabs. On the day of the big meeting at Verne's mansion, the Gagnes, along with Bockwinkel, Ray Stevens and I debated the future of the gold belt. The consensus was that it should go to me and I was flattered. I really wanted to be the heavyweight champion of the world — it's got a nice ring to it. Wearing the belt would make my childhood dream come true and allow me to fulfill my destiny and become like my hero, Bruno. But something about it just didn't strike the right chord; the timing went against everything I had learned in the old school.

The fact of the matter was the fans were expecting me to win the championship. There was no swerve, nothing surprising in that scenario. And there's nothing more important in wrestling than a good swerve. I spoke up with an idea that caught everybody off guard. There was an excellent young talent in the AWA who also had a famous wrestling ancestry. His name was Curt Hennig. I proposed we fake out the fans and put the belt on Curt in a way that would make everybody hate me even more. (Imagine, a wrestler passing up the opportunity to be champ for the good of the business.) Everyone there kinda liked the idea — but Ray Stevens loved it. He jumped up, truly excited and said he had the perfect way to make it work. And he did. He was so enthusiastic about his plans that he convinced everyone else. And so, just like that, the famous "roll of dimes" angle became part of AWA history.

When you got to know Ray Stevens you couldn't help

but love the guy. What a character. Although he was probably close to sixty when I met him, his heart and soul had never aged beyond eighteen. When it came to the wrestling business, Ray was a master. It was even a fitting coincidence that the title would change hands in San Francisco's Cow Palace — Ray's old stomping ground, the Cow Palace, had a great, old-time atmosphere and the crowd was hot.

With Bockwinkel and young Hennig ready to square off for the championship, I had sat myself down at ringside all decked out in a tuxedo to observe the festivities. The crowd grew tense, convinced I was going to do something — then the bell rang. The match between Nick and Curt started out great, and only got better. It would be hard to find anybody smoother in the ring than Bockwinkel, but Curt was also a natural. After thirty minutes had gone by in what was scheduled as a forty-five-minute-time-limit match, the fans were so into it they forgot I was even there. And once the announcer called, "One minute remaining," the crowd was convinced they were witnessing a draw. But as Curt was pulling himself up from the mat in the corner, I emerged from my chair, grabbed Curt by the hand and whispered into his ear. Although people were screaming, I slipped Curt an object. No future slow-mo videotape ever produced any hard evidence. . . .

Hennig barely made it to his feet with time remaining. And then, as Bockwinkel came up behind him, Curt turned and hit Nick with a right hand that sent the champ crashing to the canvas. With fifteen seconds left, young Curt

Hennig became the AWA heavyweight champion of the world. As I jumped into the ring to congratulate the winner, the crowd went berserk; security guards were running around in a panic, positioning themselves for the impending riot. Just then, Ray Stevens jumped into the ring. When he yanked my arm to spin me around, my hand came out of my pocket and a whole bunch of change went flying all over the ring. As Ray pointed to it, helping Nick to his feet, Curt and I were hustled out of site. For weeks afterward, Ray, Nick and the world accused me of slipping Curt a roll of dimes — and demanded revenge. I denied it, of course, on the grounds that no one had proof, that everybody, naturally, has change in their pockets.

It was a really hot angle at the time, but I'm still amazed that for years, and even today, someone will inevitably ask me whether I gave Curt Hennig a roll of dimes. And I've always given the same answer — the only thing I gave him was "the world's greatest advice."

I was having a great time in those days, but the future was bearing down on us, full speed ahead. The days of the territories were numbered. Guys like Jesse Ventura, Gene Okerlund and Bobby Heenan wound up in the WWF. When the AWA lost its national spot on ESPN, I got a call from the NWA to come to Charlotte, North Carolina, to work a program with Dusty Rhodes. It wasn't a difficult decision — if you stayed in one place too long you'd get stale. Plus, the NWA was still on the TBS superstation. Keeping up your national profile on television was what you had to do to stay on top in the world of pro wrestling. So, the next thing I knew I was in my car, driving down to Charlotte, anticipating what would become another classic feud that people would ask about for years.

The funny thing is, it never actually happened.

CHAPTER EIGHTEEN

THE KISS OF DEATH

Charlotte was the headquarters of the National Wrestling Alliance, a promotion owned by a family named the Crocketts. There was Jim, Jackie, the mother, and of course David Crockett. I enjoyed working with them — I think they respected my ability — but I was never 100 percent positive they really liked me. Actually, I think they thought, just as the fans did, that I was really an asshole. I heard some talk that a few years prior I had pissed one of them off while doing an interview. During a little feud with Tommy Rich on Georgia Championship Wrestling in the Atlanta area, a local attraction called Stone Mountain inspired a hell of an interview, giving me something I could use against the current southern hero. Stone Mountain was actually pretty cool, the world's largest chunk of granite, the size of a mountain, sticking out of the earth twenty miles east of Atlanta. One side featured a large carving — I guess it was the South's answer to Mount Rushmore. Etched into the granite, mounted on their valiant steeds, were Jefferson Davis, Robert E. Lee and Stonewall Jackson. Heroes on their horses. It was even part of a show. As the sound of Elvis singing "An American Trilogy" echoed loudly through the valley, Davis, Lee, and Jackson would triumphantly ride off the mountainside and into the heavens above. All done with lasers. The rebel yells were deafening. I could feel it even in the '80s, the spirit of the Confederacy was still alive. It inspired me and at the next TV taping I gave the southern audience both barrels. I told them I'd been to the mountaintop and that I saw the carvings of their great heroes. After I bombarded Tommy Rich with insults and threats, I made him a promise: "I'm going to beat you so bad, Rich, they're going to carve you into the side of Stone Mountain too — next to all the other great American losers!" The interview worked perfectly, the fans hated me . . . and so did some southern promoters. But they must have loved money more than they hated me, because I wasn't fired.

So, later, I was excited about doing a program with Dusty Rhodes. Not only was the American Dream one of the NWA's top guys, he could deliver great interviews. With Rhodes and myself doing promos, we'd have the crowd going nuts before we ever got to the ring. And it would all happen with great exposure on national television. The Crockett organization had a good idea in the making for a red-hot feud and topped it off with a six-foot-tall blonde, Nickla Roberts, nicknamed Baby Doll. She'd been in the NWA for a while and was involved with some of their top guys, including Dusty. It's amazing how fast time passes; I'd already been around fifteen glorious years when I first realized it was more important to be a chameleon than a wrestler. You never know what's around the corner in the wrestling business — and there I was in a different territory with a blonde valet before the karate outfits and ninjas could even collect any dust. And I was just about to collect another famous collector of dust, the Western States Heritage Championship belt.

Baby Doll was a sweet kid. The combination of her NWA escapades and my reputation made it easy to get good heat. I even got used to the fact she was taller than me. To get as much steam as they could on Baby Doll and me for the upcoming feud with the American Dream, we pulled off a short program with an up-and-coming, second-generation wrestler named Barry Windham — the son of the infamous Black Jack Mulligan, longtime tag team partner of noted bug hunter Blackjack Lanza. Barry was a great guy and excellent in the ring. Before I knew it, we were wrestling for a championship belt that materialized out of nowhere. Ironically, the Western States Heritage belt was never defended west of the Mississippi, probably never even west of Atlanta. Where else would you win the Western States Heritage championship but in Long Island's Nassau Coliseum?

Baby Doll was in my corner, and Barry and I had a memorable match. With a little help from my devious valet, the gold of the west was mine. But in terms of deviousness, the fans had not seen anything yet.

I'm amazed that for more than twenty years now, people I meet in the street still wonder about the incriminating pictures Baby Doll and I attempted to use to blackmail Dusty Rhodes. Considering Dusty's look, the minds of fans boggled at the possibilities. Just remember, the best thing you can do when wrestling on television is fire the public's imagination. I've heard every guess imaginable, from Dusty in a naked "Burt Reynolds" pose to the American Dream in drag. And remarkably, this much-talked about scenario didn't last more than three or four weeks. Baby Doll and I would come out for an interview and demand that Dusty do our bidding — or Baby Doll would show the world photos she kept in a big brown envelope, pictures that were guaranteed to ruin Dusty's life. The fans became obsessed with the angle, and I made the mistake of believing it was going to become truly huge. And profitable.

After just less than a month, the Crocketts wanted a big confrontation to occur on TV. And at the end of this public conflict they wanted Baby Doll to lay a big, juicy kiss on the Dream. It was supposed to be the kiss of death for Dusty Rhodes, but it never happened. Baby Doll walked off the set without planting the Crockett-ordered lip-lock. Of course, the Crocketts were not happy. Back then the NWA, like the AWA, were just trying to survive; it was a very bad time for insubordination.

But what the hell, who cares about things like money, success, fame, or even a career, when you're in love?

You see, Nickla was in love.

It's a funny thing, as smart as we think we are, living in modern-day society, we keep getting married. Baby Doll had recently married a young wrestler named Sam Houston — the younger brother of Jake "the Snake" Roberts. And when Sam heard his new bride was supposed to kiss Dusty on television, he went into a jealous rage. Baby Doll was so worried about ruining her marriage, she ruined her job and was promptly fired. If there were any pictures in that envelope I never saw them, and it would be another decade or so before I saw Nickla again. The mysterious pictures and Baby Doll disappeared into wrestling history. Her marriage to Sam was over in a year. But fans still ask us all about the angle that never happened.

I'm certainly no expert on love and marriage — at this time I'd just had my third son with my third and, please God, last wife. It's too bad the rest of the story never got to happen; it would have been the last classic angle of the Crockett's NWA, which was just about to go out of business. While the Charlotte-based territory had a long and distinguished existence, some of the family had finally had enough. Too much money was being lost trying to compete with McMahon. With the private jets and limos of the NWA gone, the big question was what was going to happen to the talent? In the unpredictable world of pro wrestling, one thing remained constant: if you were convinced something great would happen, it rarely did. Similarly, when you believed you were doomed, a miracle would occur.

And what a miracle it was.

Dr. Frankenstein himself would have been jealous. For what rose up out of the NWA's ashes was a larger-than-life messiah. His name was Ted Turner. What were the odds that the promotion would find a billionaire television mogul who loved wrestling?

Yes, Ted was a big fan, who also realized wrestling had been one of the highest rated shows since the beginning of TBS. And because of this, Turner was loyal to wrestling. When WTBS was a small, struggling VHF station known as WTCG, pro wrestling was the show that produced enough ratings to keep him in business, and Turner never forgot. And so Ted was going to buy what the Crocketts had to sell. In the last days of the NWA, they called everybody in for a big meeting; one of the Turner company bigwigs in a three-piece suit was about to give a talk to a room full of wrestlers. That, in itself, was a sight to behold. I don't remember much of what he said, but I'll never forget the last sentence this well-dressed man proclaimed: "It may appear at the beginning of this venture that we don't know what we are doing, but let me assure you — we do." If Turner didn't have so much money I would have almost felt sorry for him. The corporate world was now in bed with professional wrestling. The poor bastards didn't have a clue what they were getting into, God bless 'em. After the meeting, nobody knew exactly what was going on, but we agreed that whatever was going to happen would take several months. Most of the guys were simply worried about their jobs. I had another option — one that would finally make my lifelong dream come true.

CHAPTER NINETEEN

RETURN TO LARRYLAND

The '80s were almost over, and everybody seemed to know the days of the territories were over too. Everybody except Verne Gagne.

Against his accountant's advice, Verne still wasn't ready to close the doors of the AWA. Old school promoters die hard, and I guess I'm not all that different. I was with the

NWA for less than a year and there I was, another U-Haul in tow, making my way back to Minneapolis. I was starting to feel like a human going-out-of-business sale, but according to phone conversations I'd had with the Gagnes, it was finally going to be my turn to wear the gold. As the miles ticked by, running up my odometer, it was hard to wipe the smile from my face.

The reigning AWA world champion at that time was one of the many "kings" the wrestling business has produced over the years, Jerry Lawler. I had never wrestled the Memphis legend before, but I was looking forward to it. Our program should have produced some great matches, but when I arrived to fulfill my destiny, Lawler and the heavyweight championship belt were nowhere in sight. He'd fled the territory, taking the gold belt with him. This was, unfortunately, not the first or last time a champion or top guy would stab a promotion in the back. It was the oldest, most unprofessional act in the business. Not only did it hurt promotions financially, making it necessary to cancel the scheduled main event, all the talent working the territory would wind up suffering, taking the hit in the pocketbook too. Typically, these were the guys lower down on a card, who would sacrifice themselves to make the champion look good. It was always the responsibility of the main events to show up, come hell or high water — that's why they made the big bucks — because when they didn't, every other wrestler got hurt. But it takes all kinds of crazy individuals to make the wrestling business what it is. Some guys? Some guys just have no class. I felt sorry for Verne. I knew the men of the old school were heartbroken when they finally realized the loyalty of the wrestling brotherhood was a thing of the past. Surviving the contemporary business had become a true form of catch-as-catch-can. Verne and "the King" wrestled over possession of the belt until the AWA finally threatened to sue. Lawler finally complied and, after smashing the belt up with a sledgehammer, shipped the newly deformed treasure back to the AWA. This series of events led to a brand-new, and the last ever, AWA heavyweight championship belt — mine. It was a unique replica of the first-ever championship belt made for Frank Muldoon by the *Boston Police Gazette*. The big gold plate in the front was shaped like a police badge.

One fateful night, after sixteen glorious years of wishing upon a star, at the end of a brutal battle royal in the St. Paul Civic Center, in front of a sold-out crowd of Larry haters, the championship became mine. Booing thundered and echoed through the building and became music to my ears. As I stood holding up the brand-new belt, amid the throng of screaming fans, an almost indescribable feeling of accomplishment came upon me. My metamorphosis was complete: I'd achieved the ultimate and become like Bruno Sammartino. Although there have been a few times over the years I wished I had dreamed of being Donald Trump, standing in the middle of your destiny really is heaven on earth. It was such a happy place to be, I thought it only fitting to give the new home of the heavyweight champion of the world a name . . . I called it Larryland.

Inspired by a combination of Disneyland and the Griswolds' trip to Walley World in *National Lampoon's Vacation*, one by one the challengers would come to Larryland to try to relieve me of wrestling's Holy Grail, only to suffer their own custom-made "ride of doom." The list of my opponents is pretty impressive. I had some great matches with Sergeant Slaughter, and Harley Race. Nikita Koloff and Chief Wahoo McDaniel also tried in vain to capture my championship belt. I had a great feud with a former Japanese Olympic wrestler named Masa Saito. It was so good it led to a match at the second Tokyo Dome wrestling show in February 1990. We sold out the place with over 63,000 fans, outdoing Shea Stadium. It was a night to remember, but the next was just as unforgettable as the Tokyo Dome played host to another big sporting event, the Mike Tyson versus Buster Douglas fight. The Japanese wrestling promotion was gracious enough to invite the American wrestlers in town to go, and a lot of us did. We had great seats, about five or six rows behind Don King and Donald Trump. It sure felt different, sitting in the crowd looking at the ring. With the night before being so successful — when we had them hanging from the rafters — I was surprised that the Tokyo Dome was only half full. Watching Douglas and Tyson, I was comfortably squashed between the late Bam Bam Bigelow and Leon "Big Van Vader" White. Bam Bam was big enough, but Leon was bigger, maybe 6′2″ and more than 400 pounds. White was also a huge boxing fan and really excited to be there. So excited that halfway through the fight he couldn't take it anymore. The infamous Vader leaped from his seat with camera in hand and walked past the security guards he dwarfed, up to the ring apron. A second later, as he raised his camera, Tyson hit the canvas and the fight was over. Needless to say, the Tokyo Dome started buzzing. As big Leon was making his way back to his seat I noticed he was walking really slowly, like he was hypnotized. He had a blank, pale white face, like he'd just photographed the ghost of John L. Sullivan.

"Hey Leon, are you okay?" I asked.

He started mumbling, "I don't believe it, I don't believe it."

"You don't believe what?"

"Soon as I took my picture I heard Tyson say, 'Now! Now!' And then down he went."

Leon was saying Tyson took a dive. And personally, I believed him. I mean, was it just a big coincidence that less than eighteen months after the fight, Tyson's life would fall completely apart and that he'd eventually go to jail for rape?

Meanwhile, back in the AWA, the Gagnes still had one card left up their sleeves, and they wanted to present it to the new monster that was rising up out of Atlanta, Georgia — Ted Turner's World Championship Wrestling. The Gagnes' idea was a stroke of genius, and it had never been done before. What they'd come up with was the original invasion angle. With the AWA on its last legs and WCW struggling through its birthing pains, it should have been good for everybody concerned.

The plan involved the AWA invading the new WCW, led by its heel champion, me. The big match to end the program was to be world champion versus world champion — me against one of WCW's new young stars, a kid called Sting. I was really excited about the possibilities and I could have given Sting some of the best matches of his career. Unfortunately, the last card the Gagnes held was just a joker. And although the corporate bigwigs found the idea interesting, an old wrestling promoter named Jim Barnett, who acted as their consultant, scared them away from doing business with the AWA. Barnett had the old school phobia about protecting your world champion, and he told the Turner people that if Zbyszko wanted to, he could eat up Sting on live television and kill the credibility of the WCW world champion. He had a point, but that would not have been good for future business and I would never have let it happen. All we wanted to do was make money, not burn a bridge with the powerful Ted Turner. Barnett's reluctance was, however, enough to kill a great idea — for a while anyway. The invasion angle was simply ahead of its time. About seven years to be exact. It would appear again down the road and become known to all as the "New World Order." But that's a story for later. As for now, in the AWA things were coming to a crashing halt. Verne's budget was diminishing and the few big names we had left were jumping to the WWF or going over to the new WCW. Even our announcer, Larry Nelson, disappeared and left us hanging one interview day. We had to replace him on the spur of the moment with some local guy who was running around the office trying to sell rubber ninja junk and hustle his way into the wrestling business . . . . His name was Eric Bischoff.

So, whatever the AWA was trying to do by the end of 1990 was too little, and way too late. The last of the old school promoters, with dignity and grace and some reluctance, finally threw in the towel and the doors of the AWA closed forever. I consider it a great honor to be the last AWA Heavyweight Champion of the World. It's a title I'll take to the grave. As the last golden tribute to the days of territories began gathering dust next to the forgotten karate outfits and nunchuks, I was back in my car racking up more miles. This time, however, there was no U-Haul. . . .

Everything was being paid for by the Fortune 500 company that was now in the wrestling business. The Atlanta-based WCW was snatching up whatever cream of the crop was available. I was proud to be one of them. Larryland was on its way down to Turnertown and I was going to add a new attraction to my personal fantasy fun park — the WCW roller coaster. It would become the fastest and wildest ride the wrestling business would ever see.

CHAPTER TWENTY

IT'S A MAD, MAD, MAD WORLD CHAMPIONSHIP WRESTLING

After eighteen glorious years in the business, I was pretty much ready for anything. Wheeling and dealing for money and position was going to be unlike anything I'd ever experienced before. The new powers that be had transformed, and cauliflower ears became Armani suits. Instead of having business meetings in the locker rooms of assorted arenas, you were now riding the elevator up to the corporate offices of WCW in the CNN Center. I was looking forward to my first face-to-face meeting with the corporate bigwigs in charge of Turner's new enterprise. And for my part, I knew it was going to be a unique conversation. The first thing we were going to discuss was something brand new to both me and the wrestling business in general — a contract. Gone were the days of the handshake and two-weeks' notice. For wrestlers, guaranteed money over the course of a specified time would become a blessing. For the company, good intentions would evolve, down the road, into a curse. Our first fearless leader was named Jim Herd. Wearing a tailor-made suit, with well-groomed gray hair, he looked very much the corporate player. He was an okay guy and our first meeting went well: I wasn't going to do or say anything to jeopardize a guaranteed six-figures. But I was still curious about the company's game plan and about what Herd's qualifications were to run a wild and wooly business. I thought he might have come from a sports department or maybe had experience dealing with professional athletes or celebrities, where normal ranges from the clinically insane to the prima donna. Or perhaps he had a background that included running a top-rated television show.

Over the years, I became quite adept at keeping a positive poker face as my mind shrieked, "You have got to be kidding me!" This skill came in handy during that initial meeting with Herd after he told me he was brought on board after managing a string of Pizza Huts. At that very moment I knew that the new business venture I'd found myself in would be far more interesting than I could have ever imagined. Jim did appear to be an open-minded guy, however, and he surrounded himself with some experienced wrestling minds.

Ole Anderson (noted nunchuk experimentalist), who ran Georgia Championship Wrestling for TBS, was one of Herd's right-hand men. And when it came to wielding influence in a backroom situation, Dusty Rhodes was like a 300-plus-pound glob of superglue — he was impossible to get rid of.

With management and talent in place, WCW was off and running. Most of the wrestlers were hold-overs from the now-defunct NWA. Guys like Ric Flair, Barry Windham and Dusty Rhodes still figured in. Neophyte announcer Eric Bischoff and I came down from the AWA, and new faces like Lex Luger, Sting, Sid Vicious and the Steiner Brothers were becoming larger-than-life stars on the new big-screen projection TVs. One of my favorite wrestlers leftover from the Crockett era was Arn Anderson, an original member of the infamous Four Horsemen. Arn really was good. I was never big on being a tag team wrestler; I always preferred being a single competitor because they were the guys who usually became bigger stars and world champions. But when the new WCW top brass approached me with the idea of putting Arn and me together as a team called "The Enforcers," I felt we'd make a great combination. We had memorable matches together, did outrageous interviews and even in that new era still projected an old school flavor.

Arn was a fun guy and we had a great time on the road — even though in the ring I drove him nuts. He had way more of the modern bumpfest outlook than I did. The younger generation thought you needed constant movement and action, bodies always flopping around the ring. I've always believed a match should tell a story. Bouncing around the ring was great, but only after a situation was set up to make bumps meaningful. Besides, the fans were still chanting, "Larry sucks!" Even after all those years, before every match we had I would stall for as long as it took to evoke a suitable amount of chanting. Grizzly Smith, one of WCW's agents, came up to me after one match and, pointing to his watch, said, "It was sixteen minutes until the first contact." I was flattered — that had to be some kind of record. So, even though the Enforcers' matches were great, these antics would drive Arn bananas. Because he thought I would stand there like I was carved out of stone, he came up with a nickname: "Granite Man." One day, however, it was poor Arn who cracked.

Somewhere in the desert outside of Las Vegas we were doing an outdoor show at a military base. It was a miserable afternoon. The wind was ridiculous. The Enforcers were about to have a match in a sandstorm and we were not happy. We were hoping beyond hope that the entire event would be canceled, but the bleachers were already full of soldiers who for months at a time had less than nothing to do for entertainment in this God-forsaken place. As we walked out of the dressing room door I was already engaged in a severe cussing spasm. The hot, blowing sand felt like the sting of a thousand needles. We wore only trunks and boots. As we climbed onto the ring apron, we could hear the soldiers go ballistic, even though we could hardly see them through the hot brown blizzard. We just wanted to get the hell out of the storm. As the bell rang and I stepped into the ring, it happened again. The soldiers started the dreaded chant and I couldn't help myself. I started stalling. Poor Arn lost his mind. He began yelling at me, "Not today, you fucking bastard! No! No! Not now, you prick!"

I turned my head and out of the corner of my mouth said, "But Arn, they're chanting 'Larry sucks.'"

Arn screamed back at the very top of his lungs, "But they really mean it!"

I still laugh about that one. After a couple of six packs, Arn forgave me. And although he may deny it, one thing was clear — the Enforcers were a hit. Week after week we were pulling off classic antics, like breaking Barry Windham's arm by smashing it in a car door or beating up the world's strongest man, Bill Kazmaier, with his own dumbbells. I saw a good run for the Enforcers and ran an idea past Ole for a cool and captivating image. I wanted Arn and me to be on the cover of *WCW Magazine* dressed as 1920s gangsters, holding Tommy guns, surrounded by a couple of flapper girls. I thought it would have a good look for the Enforcer gimmick and so did Ole. But things really were different now. The wrestling people would always have to get approval from the corporate types. And because the suits would never make a decision that might jeopardize their jobs, they passed everything to the censorship department. The censors were not going to take any risk, so they censored everything. Needless to say, the image I had for the Enforcers was too strong for TBS. They did not like the idea of us being associated with Tommy guns — which I could never figure out, seeing how every other movie on TBS had Clint Eastwood or John Wayne armed to the teeth and shooting the hell out of somebody.

At any rate, I was beginning to see how the corporate world worked, or rather, how it shouldn't. In the early 1990s the wrestling business was stale. Too many of the same guys were being pushed too long and hard, and too many of them were over-muscled and under-talented. Everyone was clotheslining each other into oblivion. I still remember the first time Ole gave me directions to a TV taping in Albany, Georgia. "Just take I-75 south to Highway 300. It will be the huge white building with no people in it." Ole had a way with words and was mumbling a lot of them to himself when I walked into his office one day. Apparently a bunch of the contracts were up for renewal and WCW was giving big raises to the same group of guys who were not drawing money. Ole was going nuts. He told me he had just spent all morning with the corporate finance guy trying to explain that giving away all that money was not good wrestling business. Talent should be paid, he tried to explain, according to the number of tickets and pay-per-view purchases generated. The WCW approach would make a lot of the guys believe they were stars before they learned the responsibility of being on top. Ultimately, it was this very thing that produced the prima donna syndrome that would begin to plague wrestling. Just a year or two earlier, if you didn't sell tickets, you didn't eat. The funny thing is the corporate guys agreed with Ole, 100 percent. But it didn't matter.

I couldn't help but ask, "What the hell did they say?"

Ole responded in almost utter disbelief. "The chief financial officer told me that I had to spend all this money or they would think I wasn't doing my job."

God bless 'em.

When I left the office, Ole was still talking to himself and unable to recall that I was even there. Because I was one of the guys with a contract with only a couple of months to go, I couldn't wait to renew mine. I was looking forward to negotiations, especially considering the fact that Jim Herd and I had a very good business relationship. But I second-guessed myself again. I thought there would be more stability in the corporate world than in wrestling, but it was worse. No wonder all the suits were always worried about losing their jobs. Soon Jim Herd was gone and Ole had one foot on a banana peel. The Turner big shots were appointing a new fearless leader and while the new head of WCW had different qualifications than his predecessor, of course, they had nothing to do with wrestling. The guy was a corporate attorney named K. Allen "Kip" Fry. Judging by his suit, I figured he was probably a tight-ass, put there to reel in the purse strings. But, alas, six-figure contracts were still a dime a dozen and getting bigger. It turned out that our new guru was farther out than the Hubble telescope. His reasoning behind giving bigger contracts to stale talent was that because these guys were making big money they *must* be stars.

At our first meeting, Kip joyfully told me about some new ideas he had for WCW. His great ambition was to have himself thrown off a 200-foot platform attached to a bungee cord. My mental survival mode kicked in and I plastered my positive poker face on while my brain once again screamed, "Are you fucking kidding me?!"

I couldn't wait to hear his next idea . . . But when he told me, I was pleasantly surprised. WCW was bringing in some new talent in an attempt to stimulate business. It was a smart move, finally. I was still a big believer in the Enforcers and the team was over with the fans. I tried to push some of my ideas, but the new leadership already had a game plan. Their idea was to put wrestlers into groups, giving some of the new guys a rub from encounters with big-name veterans. Again, this was a pretty good idea, but I hated to see the premature demise of the Enforcers. I also did not like being part of a group — I had spent too many years building up my own reputation. One way or the other I was not going to be involved for long. The fact that the group idea would get good TV exposure for a while, along with the fact that every other Friday my checks cleared would make it easier to tolerate. As I pondered the different directions in which I could take my career, WCW matched up the Enforcers with a pre–Stone Cold Steve Austin, Bobby Eaton and the late Rick Rude along with Paul E. Dangerously, forming a very provocative group of talent called the Dangerous Alliance. And even though this collection of gifted men was getting a good push, it just wasn't my cup of tea. Combined with the fact that I was quickly approaching my twentieth year in the business, I started doing some serious thinking about hanging up the tights. Before that happened though, I wanted to pull off one more classic confrontation, one last red-hot feud fans would talk about for years. I had a great idea to run by our fearless leader. After I called his secretary to schedule the appointment, imagine my surprise when she told me he was no longer there. He'd vanished virtually unnoticed, along the lines of the Lone Ranger. Although there was no silver bullet left behind, rumor suggested the hasty exit had something to do with a desk drawer full of Prozac and sexually suggestive magazines.

I started to wonder whether I was getting paranoid or if all businesses were run by the wrong people in the right place. But whatever the case, I wasn't going to give up that easily. In the brief intermission between leaders, WCW's wrestling decisions were handled by a committee — an arrangement that always has too many agendas and never works. I ran my idea past our noble group, which consisted of guys like Ole Anderson, Jim Barnett, Dusty Rhodes, Jimmy Crockett and a handful of people who should not have been there.

The way I saw it, there were only two wrestlers in WCW (and probably the whole world) who had been around for twenty years but had never wrestled each other. Both guys were world champions, one throughout the south and one throughout the north. Both had enjoyed great exposure on national television and both had the agility to do great interviews and have great matches. They were probably the last two guys of their era who were still wrestling full-time.

Sounds almost perfect, doesn't it? There was no doubt in my mind that a confrontation between me and the wily veteran named Ric Flair would have been good business and a matchup the fans would have gotten into. And lo and behold, even the committee agreed! With their blessing, I started to compile some great interview material — and yet once again get ahead of myself. In time, I was informed that the Nature Boy had some phobia about being outshone in the ring, and that he was afraid to get into the squared circle with me. It's too bad. Over the years, I have seen insecurities and phobias prevent more good ideas from happening than the ones that did occur. But that's showbiz, and in wrestling it's always smart to have a plan B.

I just wasn't sure what that was yet.

As much as I loved what I did, the thrill of traveling throughout the country and around the world was gone. Twenty years on the road was starting to take its toll. Lady Luck had been a good friend to me — so far I'd had only two knee surgeries and one elbow operation. At forty-one, I really didn't want to push my luck much longer.

Bruno always told me there comes a time when you get too old to be taken seriously, and his words were rapidly becoming my reality. In the eyes of the promoters, I would soon start looking more like hamburger than steak. And something very strange was happening to me — I was getting a strong urge to settle down. As I had learned in the wrestling business, the card is always subject to change. I promised myself I would stop wrestling when I turned forty-five, but I was also willing to look in the mirror and renegotiate. As usual, just as I came up with a plan, destiny would intervene and take me down a road I never would have imagined. WCW was in for a big surprise too.

A new fearless leader was on the horizon . . . One who would shock the very corporate world that hired him.

CHAPTER TWENTY-ONE

THE CROSSROADS

I imagine it happens to all of us, sooner or later. One day you wake up and find yourself at the crossroads. So, which way do we go?

As I was approaching this intersection of indecision, fate stepped in and made the choice for me. I was somewhere in Indiana when it happened. After a twenty-minute match with "Big Josh" (the troubled Matt Borne in a Paul Bunyan gimmick), a miracle occurred. I walked down the three steps from the ring and when my left foot touched the floor I heard a loud "Pop!"

My left knee had blown out.

How in the hell can you wrestle twenty minutes, feel great and blow out your knee walking down three steps? It had to be a message from God. Needless to say, I was pretty upset with Lady Luck for abandoning me at ringside that night. But unknown to me at the time, that bit of torn cartilage was truly a gift from heaven: orthoscopic surgery would be a small price to pay.

Getting hurt in WCW was a pleasure. Their workers' comp insurance paid for everything and according to my contractual agreement I was looking forward to hanging around the house for a few months getting paid to rehab. For the first time in twenty years I would earn my living while injured. At the same time, back at WCW headquarters, our new commander-in-chief was moving into his fourteenth floor office. His name was "Cowboy" Bill Watts and he was easily one of the biggest assholes I've ever met in my life. A 6′5″, 300-pound, crude, vulgar man, when not talking about how tough he was, he was listening to other people talk about how tough he said he was. It was no secret in WCW that the board members of Turner Broadcasting did not want any part of wrestling. And it was only because of Ted Turner himself that they were part of the game. Now, the amount of money that was being given away was getting out of hand and the business was growing even more stale. After hearing about Watts's reputation for running a tight ship during the days of his Universal Wrestling Federation promotion in the Mid-South territory some years before, the corporate bigwigs figured he was the perfect henchman to cut spending and start turning a profit. But even without the help of a crystal ball, I could see the future of WCW's new direction. Contracts would be cut; wrestlers would be fined for being late, messing up a match, dressing badly — or anything else Watts could think of. The more money he saved, the bigger the bonus he got. God only knew what he would do to the talent roster: he lived to fire people. One sunny day as I was floating around in my pool, getting a tan and rehabbing my knee, I realized that the way WCW operated, one of two things was inevitable. Either Watts would be gone before my knee healed and I was back on active duty; or the day would come when we would have our face to face.

It wouldn't be the first time we'd butt heads. I'd had an encounter with the Cowboy some seventeen years earlier and it wasn't very pleasant. As I floated in sunny peace and quiet, I flashed back to 1975, the year I drove down to work the Florida territory. I couldn't help but notice something then: I looked a lot younger in the mid '70s and had a lot more hair to go along with my determination to conquer the wrestling business.

Bruno once again had set up the deal, by calling a friend who was running Eddie Graham's Florida territory. Enter Cowboy Bill Watts.

The arrangement was pretty simple: I was going to Florida for a short run to get a little more experience before I returned to the WWWF and a big push as Bruno's protegé. The only catch was Florida's television show played on a small station on Long Island, which could be seen in New York City. It was generally irrelevant what happened in a match in Florida — except I just couldn't be pinned on television. I had to look good for the New York/Northeast audience upon my return to the territory. When I arrived at the Florida office and met Watts for the first time, he immediately introduced me to his replacement booker, Bobby Shane. Bobby was officially taking over in a few days because the Cowboy was leaving to start a new territory called Mid-South. Actually, it was a great first day. Bobby pulled me aside and told me he wanted to give me a big push — exciting news. My Florida TV debut was just five days away and I could hardly wait. After a couple of days of reveling in my upcoming opportunity, I turned on the morning news as I was waking and I was horrified at what I saw. Surrounded by flashing lights, Sheriff's Office personnel were loading Bobby Shane's remains into the back of an ambulance. They had just pulled his body from Tampa Bay, where Buddy Colt had crashed his plane the night before. I was stunned. Days later at the TV taping, Bill Watts was back in charge, extending his stay in the Sunshine State due to the tragedy. When they passed out the TV format, I was scheduled to face the Mongolian Stomper — Florida's top heel. Well, clearly, this was either going to be a big break for me — or we were going to have a big problem.

It was not going to be a big break for me.

The agents outlining the program told me they wanted Stomper to manhandle me for two minutes, then pin me with a piledriver. I politely asked where I could locate Mr. Watts and then I was off to the big room where, seated behind a desk, was one pissed-off Cowboy.

He headed me off at the pass, before I could say anything, and threw his pencil down onto the desk. Then he cut a promo on me.

"I know what you're going to say, kid. You can't do a job because they'll see it in New York and that's what the deal was . . . Look, kid, Bruno lied to you. So if you don't want to do the job, just pack your shit and get the fuck out. I'll have to fire you."

I knew Bruno had not lied to me and I really didn't care about the concerns of the Florida territory. I was very polite in my response because I really just wanted to get out. "Thank you very much," I said, "but I simply cannot do the job."

As I left his office, Watts was yelling something to the effect of: if wrestling were a shoot nobody would be in it except him. Later that afternoon, I called Bruno and told him what had happened and that's when the shit hit the fan. He was not happy about Watts reneging on their agreement and in retaliation cancelled some bookings he had for southern promoters. This included one in Miami and one in Jim Barnett's Georgia territory. When Barnett heard that Bruno was pulling out of the first big show at Atlanta's new Omni arena, he freaked (as only Jim Barnett could).

Quickly, I learned about the power of politics and the next thing I knew, I was flying first class to Atlanta for a meeting with Barnett. He wanted to offer me a job — and of course, compel Bruno to show up at the Omni.

I walked into the dressing room early that Saturday morning. Well, it really wasn't a dressing room, just a small waiting room with a couch. WTCG was still a small VHF station at the time and its wrestling show ran on Saturday mornings at 9 a.m. Wrestlers were crammed in ball to ball, most looking like zombies after working the house show the night before. One of the boys was Bearcat Wright: he managed Abdullah the Butcher on Georgia television and also a couple of guys in Florida. He was around when Watts fired me. When Bearcat saw me, he started yelling at all of the guys in the locker room, "Hey! Wake up! Wake Up!"

Just as the wrestlers began to pay attention, Jim Barnett and Cowboy Bill Watts entered behind Bearcat's back. Without noticing them, Wright continued: "This is the guy that told Bill Watts to go fuck himself!"

Poor Bearcat just couldn't understand why he was getting absolutely no response from the other boys, who to a man simply pretended not to hear him.

I was mortified.

Then Bearcat slowly turned and discovered his hidden audience; he slumped forward, put his eyeballs back in their sockets and left the room. I accompanied Watts and Barnett to the office. While Barnett was offering me a job in his Georgia territory, Watts was trembling, staring at me like at any second laser beams would shoot from his squinting eyes and fry me where I stood. When Jim was done with his sales pitch, Watts leaned over me and, gritting his teeth, said, "Sorry I had to fire you, kid. Eddie Graham made me do it."

God only knows what Barnett had to do to get Watts to say that — although I know he didn't mean a word of it. There was a happy ending though. Bruno showed up and wrestled in the Omni. . . .

While I was lost reminiscing, there was suddenly a tremendous splash. I found myself under water, trying desperately not to aggravate my injured knee. My two younger sons had just got home from school and had tag team cannonballed me. It was just then I got a call from one of WCW's producers. Apparently, the Cowboy was hard at work cutting back on the spending. Our color commentator Jesse "The Body" Ventura had not been re-signed. Our producers were in a tight spot. They asked me if I could do some color commentary and help them out.

Believe it or not, I was almost starting to feel guilty about sitting around and getting paid so I agreed. Plus, I recognized I'd now have a whole show to talk about how great I was. Still babying my knee, I limped into the production room holding a five iron upside down and using it for a cane. (I did not want anyone thinking I was healing too fast.) Doing color seemed like an easy gig. The matches were already on tape. We'd sit in a comfortable studio chair and voice-over the action like we were there when it happened. I enjoyed it and while I was working, I heard about the Cowboy's big plans for saving WCW.

Watts had decided that everybody over forty was useless. His big brainstorm was to push a new, younger generation of wrestlers. What this really meant was that he was going to push his own kid, Erik Watts. Erik was a nice young man and a legitimate athlete, but after only three months in the business he wound up on TBS stretching an all-time great like Arn Anderson into submission. I was horrified. Even the fans wouldn't buy it. Instead of thinking that some new, nervous kid was the next big thing, everybody inside and outside the business just felt sorry for Arn.

But it was clearly the beginning of the end for ring veterans and I wasn't the only one who saw it. Ric Flair, who for some reason was champion again, fled to the WWF so fast he still had the WCW belt around his waist when he debuted on their pay-per-view. Me? I was thinking up a way to fall down the stairs convincingly so I could get another knee surgery.

Now don't get me wrong, I am all in favor of passing the torch, but there is only one way to do it: the right way, the way that is good for business. I worked too long and hard on my image and reputation to watch it get flushed down the toilet by stupid incompetence. Standing at the crossroads, my decision was becoming easier and easier.

And then, once more, the phone rang. It was my destiny calling.

Apparently, WCW's producers, after hearing my commentary, thought I was the best color man they'd ever heard. They wanted to have a meeting to see if I was interested in becoming a broadcaster.

At first, honestly, I felt insulted. After twenty years of hard work becoming the Living Legend, I was determined not to end up like Jim Ross or Tony Schiavone. Still, considering what was going on with wrestling in general, I was seriously considering an earlier-than-planned retirement. And although the guaranteed money I was making was an unheard of blessing in the business, I did not like the feeling of being owned. It was frustrating being told what to do by people who did not know what they were doing. Anyway, I was looking forward to regaining my freedom. But at the meeting with those WCW producers, I was blindsided by a disgusting low blow: they bribed me.

I was dumbfounded. They offered me more money than I made wrestling. On top of that, I would become an employee of Turner Broadcasting. This meant great benefits, health insurance and a generous 401K. Better still, it was very difficult to fire a legitimate employee, unlike an independent contractor. And all of this came for a job that required working one day a week. So much for not wanting to be owned.

I was looking forward to signing on the dotted line, but

there was a catch. The deal would have to be approved by WCW's current fearless leader — Cowboy Bill Watts.

Ah, what the hell. I never planned on being a broadcaster anyway . . .

But hey, maybe there was a chance that in the seventeen years since we'd had our showdown the Cowboy had contracted Alzheimer's and forgotten that he hated my guts. I was moving closer to finding out with each step I took down the hallway to his office. My heart started racing: half of me wanted to be cool, smooth and professional; the other half was ready for the nasty confrontation that would lead to my last day in WCW.

Now, I wasn't exactly the same quiet and respectful rookie I was in 1975. As I approached Watts's office, my cool, professional side was losing the battle. I was ready for World War III (not the pay-per-view, but the real thing). I arrived precisely at 1:59 p.m. for a 2 p.m. appointment. Just in time for Watts's secretary to inform me that he was not in.

"You gotta be kiddin' me!" I thought, "Now I gotta go through all this again!"

She was very nice though: "Mr. Watts was called over to the corporate office. Here's your new contract. It's been approved."

As she handed me the big brown envelope marked confidential, I kept waiting for Allen Funt (the old school Ashton Kutcher) to spring from a closet saying, "Smile! You're on *Candid Camera!*" It simply couldn't be this easy.

And for once, I didn't know what to say. Finally, in a smooth, professional manner, I managed, "Thank you, very much."

I walked slowly down the hall, battling the urge to run my ass off before something weird happened. By the time I got home I finally accepted that nothing weird would occur. Unlike my dealings with promoters in the past, a signed contract from Turner Broadcasting was as good as gold. Anyway, I decided to lay low, and I never went out of my way to investigate the details behind the transaction. Apparently, being an employee came under a different department, and had nothing to do with the payroll for independent contractors that Watts was shredding. And then, after a conversation with Erik Watts, I found out Bill actually liked me! I guess the Cowboy had a redeeming quality: one that was shared by a host of old school wrestlers. If you had the guts to stick up for yourself they had more respect for you. God bless the old school.

About twenty yards out my back door is a place I call the sea of tranquility — my pool. A world- and wrestling-free zone where I can think, undisturbed by the chaos of a planet gone mad. I spent some time floating around, convincing myself that I made the right decision. That people are creatures of habit is something I believe to be true. And although it wasn't easy accepting that my wrestling career was over, I wasn't stupid. I'd survived twenty years of a physically brutal occupation and could still walk around pain-free. For the next three years I would be on cruise control. All I had before me were voice-overs one day a week, and making a lot of tee times. It wasn't long before hanging up the boots started to seem like a good idea. Settling down and finally spending time with my family sounded even better. I was ready for a new adventure: the future was dead ahead and it was looking good.

CHAPTER TWENTY-TWO

PASS THE CANS

It's amazing how time flies. All of the years I spent on the road were starting to seem like a dream. Now when I wake up and look in the mirror I see a color commentator. It really is fascinating how destiny eventually brings itself into focus. When Bruno came out of retirement to wrestle me in 1980, he was doing the commentary work. My dream of becoming like my childhood hero was still evolving. And because tempting fate never worked for me in the past, when it came to wrestling with my destiny, I tapped out.

Being a perfectionist, I was determined to be the best color man I could. I did not know a lot about broadcasting at the time, but I realized that if I'd be making comments about all of the talent instead of just a single opponent, I'd need a lot more material. I bought myself a small hand-held tape recorder and started stealing every clever thing I heard. News broadcasts, song lyrics, television shows — anything and everything — were the fertile soil from whence my material grew. I never meant for the public to hear this personal collection of my nonsense, but it made my kids laugh so much that they tried to convince me to become the object of public humiliation by putting a copy of what they called *The Lost Zbyszko Tapes* in the back of this book.

Tanks, dudes.

It did not take me long to find a comfort zone in my new career. I was fortunate enough to be working with guys like Jim Ross, Tony Schiavone and "The Dean of Wrestling Announcers" Gordon Solie. They were, simply, the best play-by-play guys in the business. I learned a lot in a short time and was quickly catching on to broadcasting's unique jargon. Doing voice-overs on a pretaped show in the production room was a breeze. If you made a mistake, you just tried again. In front of a live audience, however, there was real pressure. You had to be great the first time. My first broadcast in front of a live crowd was for the *WCW*

Saturday Night show on TBS that we shot at the Center Stage Theatre in Atlanta. My partner in crime that night was Jim Ross, a guy we used to call "Spanky" because of his resemblance to Spanky McFarland of *The Little Rascals*.

But Jim was not having a good day. Bill Watts used to treat poor J.R. like a dog, always threatening to fire him. Jim showed up at the broadcast podium that Saturday a complete nervous wreck. I'm sure all those hot lights didn't help because Jim was drenched in sweat and trembling like he had an eel up his rear end. A minute before we went on, he looked over at me and in a shaky voice said, "Get the cans." I started looking around the floor for a trash can, thinking Jim needed to throw something away.

I said, "Jim, I don't see any cans."

He freaked, screaming, "The cans, the cans!"

Hey, maybe the guy needed a drink. I started looking around the podium for a soda. No luck.

"Jim, Jesus, I don't see any cans!"

I thought the poor guy was having some kind of seizure. He ripped off his headset and held them up in both hands like he was making an offering to the gods. He screamed so loud that our floor director, well, hit the floor: "THE CAAAANNNNNSS!!"

I finally got it.

"Oh. You mean the headsets."

After the taping, an exhausted and soaked Jim Ross came up to me and apologized for being such a maniac. He confessed the Cowboy was driving him crazy. I felt sorry for

Spanky — and everybody else in WCW. But good news was right around the corner. I heard rumors that the corporate big shots who brought Watts in had realized they'd made a mistake shortly after they hired him.

Big business works like this: if you fire the person you hire too fast, you look like the idiot. The Cowboy was given enough time to gather plenty of rope — more than enough to hang himself.

The bigwigs were horrified during the corporate meetings where Watts would come in wearing blue jeans and cowboy boots, bellowing vulgarities. And when Bill did not feel like walking down the hallway to the men's room, he simply opened the sliding door to the small balcony of his twelfth-floor office to whiz over the rail upon the pedestrian ramp below. Needless to say, the suits were mortified. The *coup de grace* came in the form of an interview Watts did with the *Pro Wrestling Torch Newsletter* that was something less than flattering to African-Americans. When a reporter for the *Pittsburgh Post-Gazette* named Mark Madden sent a copy of it to Hank Aaron, who was on the Turner board, it was all they needed to send the Cowboy riding off into the sunset.

Standard operating procedure after firing a fearless leader was putting together a committee. This time guys like Greg Gagne of the AWA Gagnes, Bill Dundee, Mike Graham and Kevin Sullivan would be keeping the ship afloat while the big shots drew up a new plan — one that wouldn't jeopardize their jobs.

I began spending a lot of time in the sea of tranquility with my kids and going on a lot of dinner dates with my wife. I was playing so much golf I actually got pretty good at it. I hadn't realized how much I'd love being a broadcaster. No more traveling to a different city every day just to get punched and kicked in the face by another big, sweaty, brutal, dumb bastard . . . What in the hell was I thinking for the past twenty years? I loved my new destiny, and I was having the time of my life, working with some of the classics.

Gordon Solie was the last survivor of an almost forgotten era. He came from the world where wrestling commentary was a one-man show. Talking slowly and always seriously, he mastered the art of creating drama and bringing to life what you saw on the screen. I learned a lot about broadcast psychology from "the Dean." Before our afternoon voice-overs, we would meet at Reggie's Pub, a restaurant in the CNN Center. I would have the fish and chips and Gordon would have a few drinks and a pack of cigarettes. He was quite the character. After lunch, he'd put on the cans and make the fans believe.

Most people don't quite realize how important a good broadcast team is. Working with WCW's talented trio left me constantly amazed at their ability to never run out of bullshit. I did a lot of the syndicated shows with Tony Schiavone. These programs were pre-edited and just needed voice-overs. It was not easy being witty and entertaining at the same time. So many of the matches were all too similar.

The new wrestling mentality was suffering from what I called "clickerphobia." The powers that be were convinced that people would switch to a different show, without leaving their sofa, the second things slowed down. There had to be constant action.

Grabbing a hold on someone in the middle of the ring would send the office into a frothing panic. Wrestlers were not even tying up anymore. Match after match, one guy would be in the ring when his opponent would run down the ramp, slide under the bottom rope and then start a furious brawl. After a minute of this meaningless slugfest, the over-pumped and under-seasoned performers would start running around the ring, bombarding each other with a bevy of clotheslines. It seemed like every other move was a clothesline — or a "modified clothesline" if they missed the spot. Half of the commentary went like this: "Wow! What a clothesline! Wow! What a clothesline! Oh! He ducked the clothesline! Bam! What a clothesline!"

It was so bad, I began dreaming clotheslines in my sleep. (And when was the last time anyone used a real clothesline, anyway? I mean, to dry clothes? Most of the kids watching had no idea what a real clothesline was.) It was becoming so ridiculous, I found myself begging the office to tell the talent to stop with the clotheslines, already. They needed to force the boys to do something else so the matches would at least be different.

Their response was hard to argue with: "Most of our new superstars don't know any other moves."

So, as much as I enjoyed doing commentary, "Clotheslinemania" was getting on my nerves. No wonder the business was stale.

I had to come up with an idea that would break the monotony for myself and everyone else in the production room. And I came up with a great one: gambling.

Before we'd get down to work, I would look over the lineup and make a rough guess at how many clotheslines would be thrown during the show. This would depend on who was booked for the matches. If guys like the Public Enemy or the Nasty Boys were scheduled, I had to add at least ten extra clotheslines to the over/under. Everyone from the sound guy to the makeup girl would place their bets and take their chances. And while it made a day in the audio booth much more enjoyable, I sometimes wondered if I opened Clotheslines Anonymous whether our talent would sign up for group therapy.

But sadly, that would never happen. The new generation of stars went from pumping up biceps to big contracts. They missed the part about learning your trade and paying your dues . . . . They just believed they were stars.

There was a popular joke that circulated throughout the wrestling business for years, which went: What would you do if you had two million dollars? The punchline? I would wrestle until it was gone.

It's sad but true. Once wrestling gets into your blood you're hooked forever. Even after accepting the fact that I was a retired wrestling addict, I would still get the occasional urge to put on the tights. My fix showed up one day at TBS in the form of a British wrestler named Steven Regal. He was a very talented young man who had the unique ability to piss off the crowd by just standing there. He reminded me of me. And he had only one drawback: he could actually wrestle. Accordingly, our committee couldn't figure out what to do with him. There was no one they could book Regal with who could keep up with him in a wrestling match.

In this new era, Regal was one of only a handful who carried on the tradition of the old school that had all but died. I found myself unable to sit, content, betting on the clothesline over/under while this great talent wasted. When this was combined with the fact that I couldn't get my message across that too many clotheslines were spoiling the broth, I saw my chance to prove my point by example.

Taking advantage of the fact that our ratings could use a boost, I laid out a scenario the committee just couldn't resist. Regal produced such natural heat that building up a week-to-week, episodic program was a no-brainer. Really, all I did was rearrange the angle that Bruno and I had pulled off in 1980. The first step was to elevate Steve Regal to royalty. He would now be known as Lord Steven Regal and be accompanied by his servant, Sir William (also known as Memphis veteran superstar Bill Dundee). Like my mentor, I was now doing the color commentating and every time I went to interview the snobbish Lord Regal I would be arrogantly ignored. All it took was a few weeks of this simple but effective buildup before I made my stand and insulted his royal highness.

Although the fans loved it, it infuriated his lordship and he demanded an apology. Me begging for forgiveness was never going to happen, but a match on *WCW Saturday Night* certainly could. The timing of this confrontation was perfect and proved my point. The Memorial Day weekend sweeps period was the hardest time for us to pull a good rating. I was really looking forward to this match with Lord Regal and because of my strenuous one-day-per-week schedule, I managed a few workouts in between golf games. For a forty-two-year-old guy who never took steroids I still looked pretty good.

The big day finally arrived and the evil Lord Regal made his way to the ring. He looked more like royalty than Prince Charles. When I made my appearance, a pleasant surprise filled my cauliflowered ears: the crowd was chanting my name so loud that Center Stage was trembling. This time the chants of "Larry!" that echoed through the arena weren't followed by the word "sucks!"

I was a babyface!

Without sounding like I'm bragging, this really was the best technical wrestling match of my career — and one of the best WCW had ever seen. They say it takes two to tango; I do not know how to dance, but it certainly takes two to have a great match. I was an excellent ring technician and Regal really was absolutely great, the best wrestling heel at that time. We put holds on each other that the boys had never seen before. When Tony Schiavone and Bobby Heenan did the voice-overs the next day, I had to sit in with them because they did not know the names of some forgotten holds we'd used, like the surfboard, or the standing, reverse figure four. It was a shame that a talent like Steve Regal was considered less important than the gassed-up, clotheslining buffoons, but that night we proved them wrong. The wrestlers raved about the match as much as the fans. The late Brian Pillman called it a twenty-seven-minute wrestling clinic and he was right. The boys did not believe a match could be that good and go so long without so much as one clothesline. The office was astounded too. They found it hard to believe that a mid-card character (in their eyes) and a color commentator could produce the highest rating TBS ever had during the May sweeps — but they had to take notice because it was true. I had not felt that self-satisfied since Shea Stadium.

But I also felt something else: pain! I was never so sore in my life. Even though I went to the gym on a regular basis, my body just wasn't used to wrestling anymore. For a week, I could barely walk. I hurt everywhere. A couple of European uppercuts bounced off my chest and had cracked two of my teeth. My great idea of putting on a wrestling clinic for the boys cost me $2,500 for crowns. But in a sick, wrestling way, it was worth it.

After a couple of weeks of living in a hot tub, life began to return to normal. My broadcasting career was moving full steam ahead and I was spending most of my time right where I belonged: on the golf course. I couldn't imagine life getting much better, but destiny was about to prove me wrong once more. A disturbance was brewing in the force, a series of events so unpredictable that Nostradamus himself could not have seen it coming. . . .

Professional wrestling was about to become huge — bigger than it had ever been (and probably bigger than it will ever be again).

This explosion made the Haystacks Calhoun calamity seem like indigestion.

CHAPTER TWENTY-THREE

THE LAST WORLD ORDER

By the time 1996 rolled around, it was hard to believe that twenty-three years had passed since I'd gotten my start. Besides counting the years, I was also counting blessings. In more than two decades I'd suffered only five surgeries and a mouthful of crowns. My one big fear was having my two front teeth knocked out but that never happened. My feud with Lord Regal had provided enough of a fix to allow me to hang up my boots in peace. I was never the kind of person that was willing to sell his soul to play the game of life, the kind that says, "He who dies with the most money wins." I was perfectly satisfied doing color commentary: it kept me in the business I loved and I was getting more exposure than most of the wrestlers. Besides, most guys my age were already gone.

I wound up doing quite a few shows: the Saturday morning *WCW Pro* program, *WCW World Wide* and the syndicated *WCW Pro* shows. I also did all of the international market shows.

We used those international shows to develop some new play-by-play announcers. I wound up breaking in guys like Chris Cruise, a moonlighting federal investigator named Scott Hudson, and the guy at ringside when Colonel DeBeers thought he had relieved Kerry Von Goofball of his foot, Mike Tenay. Another B-team announcer that was running around the production room was an old buddy from the AWA, Eric Bischoff. One day he asked me to wish him luck because he was applying for a new position in WCW, executive producer.

There were some other people excited about the prospects of getting this job as well: men who had toiled for years behind the scenes in World Class Wrestling from Texas and the WWF had thrown their hats into the ring. I wish I had known what that position would have evolved into, because I would have invented a resume myself. We thought it meant being in charge of production, but a miracle would soon happen that produced WCW's last, but by no means least, fearless leader.

One might be inclined to think that the corporate guys would've selected the candidate with the most experience in producing a television show. . . . But no, they hired the guy who used to sell rubber ninja gimmicks out of his trunk.

And they had no idea how lucky they were.

They finally had picked the right guy at the right time. The winner of the "Let's See Who Can Make Up The Best Resume Contest" was unquestionably Eric Bischoff. It's times like this that make me remember the old saying: "Be nice to everyone on your way up, because you may meet them on your way down."

Back in the AWA when Eric was trying to work his way into the business, he told me he wanted to be a pilot so I used to take him flying. We had a great deal of mutual respect for each other. This would come in handy when he needed my advice down the road. Eric had all the qualities of a good promoter. Aside from being a good hustler, Bischoff could lie, cheat, intimidate, promise, beg, hold his breath and cry at will. In time, he would need all of these skills — and more.

WCW's biggest fan, Ted Turner, decided it was time to wake the sleeping lion. He wanted WCW to outdo the WWF and become number one. All the big shot yes-men quickly agreed and took themselves out of the line of fire by putting their executive producer in charge of Ted's new pet project.

Turner wanted a show on Monday night, opposite the WWF, and unlocked the vault to make it happen. I remembered the meeting we had years earlier, when the Crockett family was selling out to Turner and the man in the three-piece suit said, "You may not think we know what we are doing, but let me assure you, we do."

I finally saw the light.

They did not know what they were doing, but they had enough money to do whatever the hell they wanted. Enough cash, in fact, to create the hottest, highest-rated show in cable television.

WCW Monday Nitro was about to be born.

Bischoff and the committee, along with a top-notch production department, started laying the groundwork for Ted Turner's new vision. Their first brainstorm was to bring in a wrestler that just about everyone in the free world had heard of, Hulk Hogan. In terms of generating some buzz before the birth of a new show, it was a great idea. They gave the Hulkster their best shot, the red carpet treatment. . . . They held a red and yellow tickertape parade through the streets of Disney World.

The only problem was nobody cared. Hulk's limited in-ring ability was becoming old news. Loyal wrestling fans were booing Hogan because he reminded them of the WWF. Bischoff was, to say the least, not thrilled with this and he started an internal campaign to prevent any of the negative comments from reaching the upper echelon. He ran through the company, telling everyone that if they didn't think that bringing in Hulk Hogan was an act of sheer genius, a "ten," they were free to quit. People got the hint.

It became a running joke throughout the office: "What did you think about Hogan's awful match last night?"

"It was great! Fantastic! He's still got it! It was a ten!"

It was clear that with *Nitro* locked in a ratings war with the WWF, WCW would need something more. As you'll remember, Bischoff, Greg Gagne and I were leftovers from the AWA. Some years earlier we were disappointed that the "invasion of WCW" angle had never come to fruition. But with Turner Broadcasting throwing money around like they had a printing press in the basement, there was no reason we couldn't make it work now.

A little more than a decade earlier, Vince McMahon, Jr. broke with tradition and snatched away top talent from the other territories in his attempt for wrestling supremacy. The rest of the wrestling world, through WCW, was about to get payback — in wrestling terms, a receipt.

Mysteriously (and admittedly, a little shadily), Scott Hall, Kevin Nash and Sean Waltman had not re-signed their deals with the WWF. It was a case of history repeating itself. This time, WCW snatched up the WWF's top guys. You can just imagine how elated McMahon was at this development. The "Monday Night War" between the WWF and WCW was becoming the hottest angle the fans had ever seen. Clickerphobia was becoming Clickermania. Quickly, Monday night belonged to professional wrestling and at times the combined ratings of the companies would dwarf those of the NFL.

Now, we had everything we needed to make it look like the WWF was invading WCW.

Even the psychology of human nature was on our side. We were the underdog. The new kid. Number two. The WWF was seen as the long-established bully. All WCW had to do was program everything right and we'd obtain maximum results. (And I humbly add, this is where my help was needed.)

It happened in Macon, Georgia, during a production meeting before a live *Nitro* broadcast. It was going to be the beginning of the invasion angle — and Scott Hall's first appearance.

But Eric Bischoff's original idea was actually pretty flat.

At the meeting, he laid out his plan for Hall to just sit at ringside. Our cameramen were supposed to get casual shots of him — as if fans wouldn't recognize a huge WWF star sitting in our crowd. After outlining his idea, he asked if everybody liked it. Of course, everyone did.

I hated to bury him in front of thirty employees but that idea wouldn't work. When he saw me shaking my head in disapproval, he let out a slow, agonized "What?" — like he knew what was coming.

I reminded everyone that this was supposed to be an invasion. An attempted takeover by big, mean, nasty, evil guys who hated us for taking their Monday time slot. I suggested we have a normal match when, out of the blue, Scott Hall, a WWF guy, would hit the ring and purposefully disrupt our show. It had never been done before and it would shock the wrestling world. When Scott grabbed the microphone, we would have our director go nuts and our security lose their minds trying to get rid of him — make it look real. This would set the stage for Hall, Kevin Nash and Sean Waltman, down the road, to bust into control rooms, locker rooms and through the broadcast table. Now, that's an invasion.

Eric loved it.

Then, of course, so did everyone else.

It was hot. It was great. It was a "ten."

Wrestling would no longer be stale: we had the hottest angle the world will ever see. In appeal and in ratings, WCW quickly became the top dog. The WWF was a distant second.

There really was a New World Order.

The NWO faction got so huge it became a challenge to keep people out of it. Every wrestler with half a brain wanted to jump on this gravy train. Even Hogan realized the only way to keep the Hulkster in the limelight was to go Hollywood and join the dark side. The New World Order, led by an old pro named Ted DiBiase, was pushing merchandise through the ceiling. It seemed like every other person on the planet was wearing an NWO T-shirt: the phenomenon was getting so big so quickly that even our fearless leader could not resist the temptation . . .

DiBiase was sent home and, you guessed it, Eric Bischoff was the new leader of the NWO.

Business at that time really was unbelievable. Twenty-thousand-seat arenas around the country were selling out within an hour of tickets being offered for sale. We had it all: the biggest names of the recent past (Hogan, Macho Man Randy Savage, Rowdy Roddy Piper), the colorful new daredevils called *luchadores* and a group of dancing beauties we called the Nitro Girls.

WCW could do no wrong. Everything we did got over and became a pop-culture trend: smashing limos; dropping wrestlers safely from the ceiling; Mean Gene and the Nitro Girls showing up at your house and broadcasting your *Nitro* party to the masses. . . . *WCW Monday Nitro* was the most exciting thing to happen to TV since color. And I got to be smack dab in the middle of it.

Destiny was closing in from all sides when it made me an offer I could not refuse.

CHAPTER TWENTY-FOUR

A HAPPY ENDING (NO, NOT THAT KIND)

As silly as this might sound, I loved being a professional wrestler. It took a unique individual to reach the top and withstand the test of time. It's too bad the stigma of being "fake" kept us little devils from collecting our due. . . .

To put on a physically brutal show, sometimes for sixty minutes, one had to be extremely athletic, in tremendous shape. To take bone-shattering bumps and fly through the air, you had to be an acrobat. You were a writer for interviews and a choreographer during your matches. To make the fans love you or hate you, you had to be a psychologist. It took a special kind of person, one who was completely fearless. And the energy of 20,000 screaming people going through you, that adrenaline rush, was addictive. I still loved being in the business and sitting in the middle of everything, with Tony Schiavone and Mike Tenay, sitting next to the ring at the broadcast table, putting on the cans and bringing the show to life. Surrounded on all sides by a sea of heads and smartass signs, we had the best seat in the house.

During one *Nitro* pandemonium finally prevailed — fans went ballistic and all hell broke loose. The NWO was in the ring. Scott Hall, Kevin Nash, Hulk Hogan and Eric Bischoff were strutting around, doing their weekly routine and pissing off the crowd. When they finished creating their Monday madness by threatening to take over WCW, the live broadcast stopped and we went to a commercial break.

Nash, Hogan and Bischoff were leaving the ring when Scott Hall leaned over the top rope and pointed his finger at me. When he started bad-mouthing me, I stood up and threw off my cans. The fans exploded.

The thunderous pop, which no one saw coming, was so loud that Nash, Hogan and Bischoff threw their hands over their heads and ducked like there was incoming artillery. When my golf ball–sized eyes met Scott Hall's golf ball–sized eyes, we knew what had to happen. The fans had just booked it for us.

There was no way in hell Scott Hall and I were not going to have a match.

Everybody in the business heard the sound of money.

The *Monday Nitro* commentary came in two shifts. I did the color on the first hour and one of the funniest men alive, Bobby "The Brain" Heenan, did the second. Normally, I'd be at the nearest casino before the show was over, but that night I went straight to our fearless leader. Bischoff was dumbstruck by the intensity of the crowd reaction; it had just scared the crap out of him. It took about a second to convince Eric I had to put the boots on again. But he was in for another surprise: I was going to wrestle him first.

Okay, it took about two seconds to talk him into that. I was going to program this angle differently than anyone expected. The fans wanted to see me wrestle Scott Hall, so I decided to make them wait. In time, they'd want it more. In the ensuing weeks, I booked scenarios where Scott Hall would be making fun of me and cracking wise about how I was so out of it that I could not beat up "Easy E," a.k.a. Eric Bischoff. Bischoff would follow up by bragging about what a dangerous karate killer he was. In the meantime, in their effort to take over WCW, the NWO was continuing to grow in numbers, adding guys like Scott Norton, Buff Bagwell, Vincent and the late Bryan Adams, as well as some corrupt referees.

This Monday night wrestling soap opera was becoming hotter than the sun. Fans were mesmerized and even wrestlers were astounded. Diamond Dallas Page took me out to dinner to pick my brain about creating hot angles . . . but he hadn't seen anything yet.

The next few weeks would see the NWO wreaking havoc. They disrupted everything. When I tried to stand up for WCW, a group of them would attack me and hold me down while Bischoff — without any rubber ninja gimmicks — assaulted me with vicious karate kicks. The following week we dropped thousands of 8 x 10's from the ceiling: photos of Bischoff standing over my unconscious body. Eric was getting so much heat, fans were jumping the rails and busting security to take shots at him.

It was just like the good old days.

Things were reaching a fever pitch. The fans made it clear they wanted me to beat the hell out of Bischoff and then get my chance with Scott Hall. More than anything else, that would be the money match. At the beginning of every *Nitro*, the sold-out arena would chant "Larry! Larry!" until I stood up from the broadcast position to give them the "big L" salute.

But I was getting a lot of heat too. Not from the fans — from the stars.

A few of our top babyfaces were upset that a color commentator was more over than they were. I found the jealousy flattering. I did not care about them anyway: all I cared about was me and the fans. And I was about to give them what they wanted. I accepted Scott Hall's challenge: if I could beat "Easy E," then Hall agreed to face me in the ring. The fans were drooling.

The match was set for our big pay-per-view, "Starrcade," on December 28, 1997, in Washington, D.C. We added a special stipulation to put things over the top. If Bischoff could beat me, the Living Legend, then the NWO would gain control of *Nitro*. The drama was so intense I could hardly stand it myself. The bigger the expectation, the better the match had to be to satisfy our rabid fans. Being the perfectionist I am, I realized this was going to take some work. Bischoff was getting great heat, but he had never really been in the ring. The pay-per-view was only four weeks away. Because "Eazy E" was the incumbent fearless leader, we had no problem getting the keys to the infamous WCW Power Plant training center. We decided to meet there a few times late at night to go over the match so Eric could get the routine down.

The first session went fairly smooth. Eric could pull off a believable cocky bastard persona and had some decent martial arts moves. I could work around everything else. It was going better — and more easily — than I expected.

The next time we met the match was shaping up nicely. While we were playing around with a few moves, Eric tried to get cute and put a hold on me. I countered and when I went to take him down, wouldn't you know it, he blew out his knee.

Holy shit! There goes the pay-per-view. I was horrified.

As our fearless leader was limping around in agony, I was watching my big program go up in smoke — "Starrcade" was only a couple of weeks away. We called it quits. Eric went off to have knee surgery and I went home to await the verdict. How could this have happened? Everything was going so well! The fact that I broke the boss's leg did not bother me that much. But the upcoming pay-per-view had a chance to do a monster buy rate. The biggest in history. Our match and the inevitable Hulk Hogan versus Sting match made this the most anticipated pay-per-view ever. Somehow, it just had to happen.

The next day I received news that lifted my spirits. Eric did not require surgery. Swelling and a little cartilage damage was something we could all live with.

Hallelujah!

Bischoff was determined to have his knee ready for "Starrcade." I felt great. At forty-six, I could still bench 365 pounds.

When you are in a state of anticipation, two weeks fly: "Starrcade" was upon us. Butterflies were multiplying in my stomach. Would Eric's knee hold up during the match? Would it go the way we planned?

Merely having a good match was not an option; I really wanted to steal the show. To make sure Eric's lack of ring experience would not be noticed, and to add more tension, we added Scott Hall to Eric's corner and put Bret "The Hitman" Hart in as special referee. He would keep the match on the up and up. Or would he? Could I save *Nitro* from the New World Order?

The drama was tremendous, and fans were literally on the edges of their seats. Bischoff and Hall were making their way to the ring and then it was my turn. When I made my entrance, they were playing my song: the *Nitro* theme. The MCI Center went absolutely nuts. I had not heard a crowd that emotionally intense since Bruno walked into Shea. I was in heaven as I walked toward the ring, destiny at my side. The NWO did not have a chance.

Bischoff tried in vain to get the upper hand, using every martial arts trick he knew. To no avail. When I tossed him around like a rag doll and rubbed his face in the canvas, the roof nearly came off the building. Even Scott Hall's attempts at interference were thwarted. The chants of "Larry! Larry!" shook the arena to its foundation. When Bret Hart raised my hand in victory, the noise was indescribable. I had saved *Nitro* from the New World Order and we had set the table for the next pay-per-view. At "Souled Out" I would face my arch-enemy, the 6′4″, 300-pound grease man, Scott Hall.

Scott did a great job as the top bully of the invading army trying to take over WCW. Unlike the inexperienced, corrupt executive, Hall's imposing presence was that of a seasoned veteran. This time, instead of saving *Nitro*, I would be trying to save myself.

The problem with giving top guys guaranteed contracts is that it usually comes back to bite you in the ass. In WCW, some of the biggest stars wound up not doing what the office wanted them to do because they had nothing to lose. Aside from Hall and me, one of the top matches was scheduled to be Bret Hart versus Ric Flair. Hulk Hogan would not be a part of the show, however. For some reason, he wanted to prove that Bret Hart was not a big draw on pay-per-view — but his timing was awful. The New World Order angle was so hot that a marquee card was irrelevant. The buy rate would be through the roof, regardless.

What a wonderful time it was. For a while we captured the emotions and the imagination of the wrestling world. And even the old school raised itself from the dead for a brief, cameo appearance. The ghosts of Stanislaus Zbyszko and Strangler Lewis had to be proud as they watched me and Scott Hall, battling in the name of tradition and for the honor of WCW.

I really believe we stole the show. Another 20,000 strong produced enough emotional energy to topple the walls of Jericho (no, not him) and bring another mega arena to its knees. It was as close as a dreamer like me can get to heaven on earth.

As I made my way up the ramp and emerged under the spotlight of the biggest, hottest, highest-rated television show the wrestling world had ever seen, thousands of purple and yellow balloons, the colors of WCW, dropped from the ceiling to rain down around me. With millions and millions of people watching worldwide, those thunderous chants hit me like a ton of bricks.

After all these glorious years and adventures, my dream

was finally reality. As the ring announcer introduced me as wrestling's "Living Legend," I knew that destiny had granted the wish of the young boy I was long ago. I'd become just like my hero — a good guy, who was once the heavyweight champion of the world, a legendary figure who came face to face with evil and stood victorious.

You could not argue with the numbers: the buy rates for "Starrcade" and "Souled Out" were the biggest in the history of WCW.

And there was a beautiful damsel in distress to save as well. . . .

Her name was *Monday Nitro* and the New World Order would never put her in danger again.

WCW and the NWO had their own, different destiny. One that even great ratings couldn't change. Both would soon be "sold out" by the corporate world. When Time Warner killed WCW by selling it to McMahon, it was "paradise lost" for professional wrestling. The usual suspects and self-appointed wrestling experts would point fingers for months, spreading useless opinions, rumors and innuendo via countless newsletters and websites. Some have even written books on the subject.

But it really wasn't all that complicated.

Yes, WCW was a tangled mess in the end. And sure, the inmates were running the asylum. But WCW was always a mess. Among all the puppets and scapegoats, there was only one truly fearless leader.

When AOL bought out Turner/Time Warner, Ted Turner

lost his stroke. AOL did not want anything to do with wrestling — and the corporate bigwigs did not want to lose their jobs. Unlike the WWE, which is a wrestling company, WCW was just a cable network television show. I'm amazed it lasted as long as it did.

It was hot, it was great, it was a ten. . . .

Or was it that destiny just didn't need WCW anymore, once my dreams had come true?

When it was over, I walked to my backyard sea of tranquility to ponder this very question. By my side was my loyal, 85-pound canine companion: a boxer named "Bruno."

As I floated around my pool, basking in the sun and the glory, I was completely detached from the real world.

I never could figure out what's so important about reality anyway. There's only one future — old age and death. So why not live a dream?

Unlike Alexander the Great, who wept when he felt there were no new worlds to conquer, I indulged another ambition . . . I could not wait to try my luck at golf — on the professional seniors tour. And then, a few months later I took a call from a group called Total Nonstop Action or TNA — a new wrestling company, with a dream of their own.

ABOUT THE PHOTOS

Photos 9-13 and 18-28 of the photo section are courtesy of George Napolitano.

All others are from the collections of Sharon Freeman or ECW.

The photos opening chapters 2; 4-6; 11; 13-14; and 16-20 are courtesy of George Napolitano.

The photos opening chapter 9 and 21-22 are courtesy of Mike Lano.

All others are from the collections of Sharon Freeman or ECW.